THE
STORY OF
25
EVENTFUL
YEARS
IN PICTURES

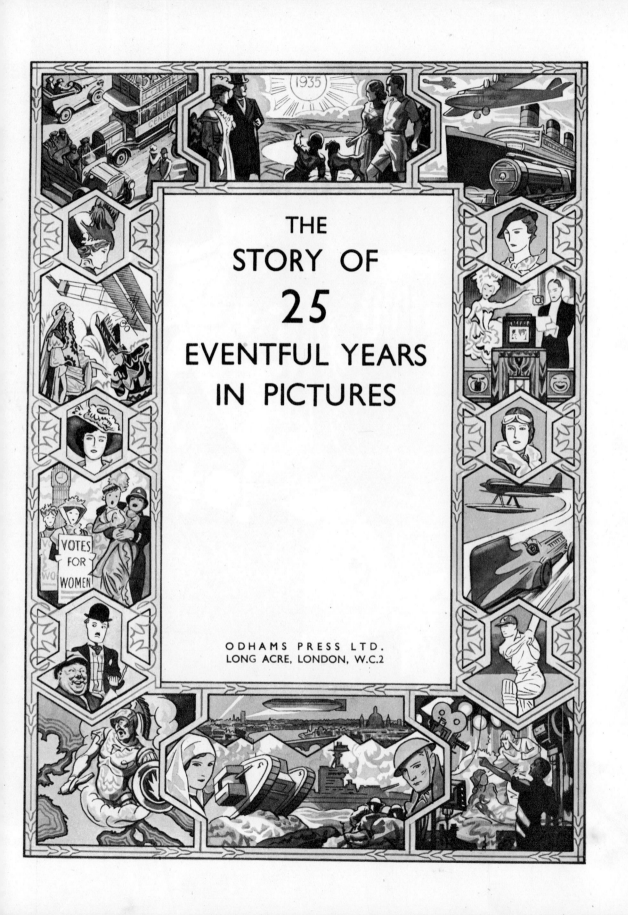

THE
STORY OF
25
EVENTFUL YEARS
IN PICTURES

ODHAMS PRESS LTD.
LONG ACRE, LONDON, W.C.2

THEIR MAJESTIES KING GEORGE

QUEEN MARY

Command photographs specially taken
to commemorate the Silver Jubilee

H.R.H. THE DUKE OF GLOUCESTER

H.R.H. THE PRINCE OF WALES

H.R.H. THE PRINCESS ROYAL

Photo : Bassano

H.R.H. THE DUKE OF YORK

H.M. THE KING   H.M. THE QUEEN   H.R.H. THE DUKE OF KENT

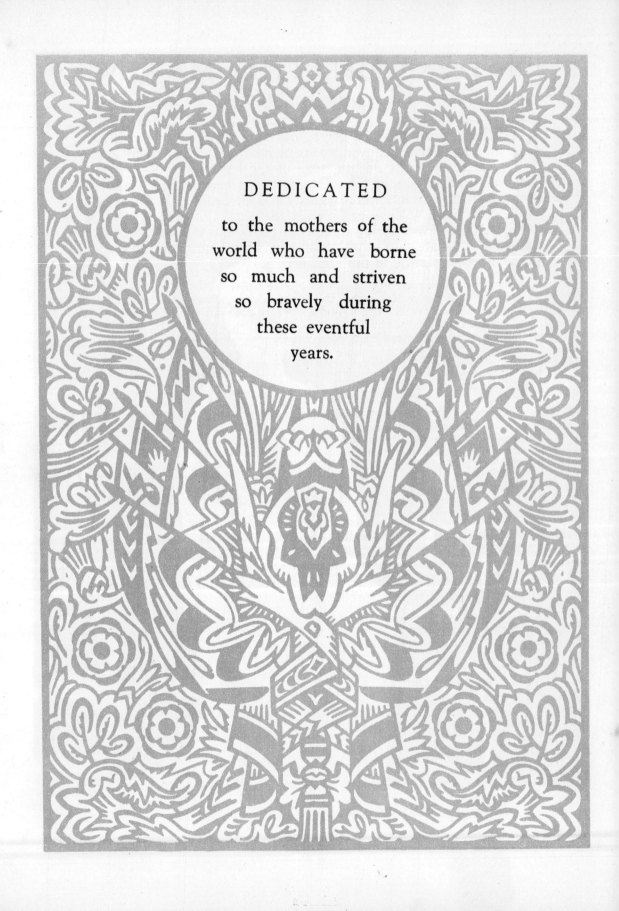

DEDICATED

to the mothers of the
world who have borne
so much and striven
so bravely during
these eventful
years.

HISTORY IN THE MAKING
1910 to 1935

NEVER, since the world began, has so much been achieved, such an abundance destroyed, so many hearts lifted, so many hopes denied, as in the fleeting span of the last quarter-of-a-century. Each year in the reign of King George V has been an act in a drama almost incredible in its speed, intensity and incident. They have been tremendous times. None can predict the verdict of posterity, but all those who have lived during these eventful, fateful years, must be conscious that they are themselves a part of history, sharing in the shaping of the ultimate destiny of the human race.

These yesterdays are not dead. They live again in the pages that follow. Their vitality is preserved in pictures that convey a story no words can tell. History is given the human touch. The episodes of peace and war, the happiness and the heartbreak, the high-lights and the shadows of the past, are here irrevocably bound up with the lives and aspirations of every citizen.

The reign of King George V has been an age within an age. Progress has bounded ahead with awesome purpose, smashing ruthlessly the conventions of centuries. Man has accomplished his final conquest of the air. He flies faster and farther than the birds fly. He has explored the secret fathoms of the sea; peeped into the scorching mouths of volcanoes and he has filled the air with voices and song. Ships with streets of shops sail the merchant routes. Australia, eleven thousand miles away, has been brought within three days of the Motherland. Petrol, oil and electricity work their daily miracles.

Even if we forget all else but the startling advance of radio, aircraft, X-ray, the gramophone, and talking picture, the motor-car and the newspaper, enough has been accomplished to warrant these years being acclaimed a wonder period of history.

But that is not all. The entire fabric of our lives has been changed by all this restless evolution. Science and medicine have been sleepless in their vigilance. Many deadly enemies of the human body have been discovered and destroyed.

In industry working conditions have in a number of ways been brightened and simplified though much yet remains to be done.

Sport and recreation have come into their own. Mighty football stadiums, playing fields and open spaces, palatial cinemas and concert halls have brought facilities for passing the leisure hours within the reach of all.

Women have won a new freedom. The tyranny of fashion is ended. The drudgery of housework has been mitigated. Women vote. They sit on the green benches at Westminster. Their lives are fuller.

But see for yourself! See all the magic and movement of these years in a pageant of pictures that will never fade from your memory. The curtain rises on the funeral of King Edward VII. Nine kings and thirty princes followed the cortege to the Royal tomb at Windsor. The Kaiser, so soon to be a central figure of the world war, rides in the van.

The Peacemaker has passed on. And the same year—1910—the first British

Army airship reared its clumsy head, a grim symbol in the sky of the death and destruction that was later to hurtle down from above.

The year 1911 was filled with glamour. It was imbued with hope, sealed with celebration.

At home in England, King George V was crowned amid scenes of beauty and splendour.

The shy, solemn Prince of Wales, in his robes of State, was presented to the people of Wales at Caernarvon Castle with all the traditional colour and ceremony dating back to King Edward I.

The last horse-drawn motor-bus left the streets, women played golf in huge cloth caps and tripped over trailing skirts at tennis, hand-painted stockings were a sensational fashion vogue, and John Bunny and Flora Finch were the film stars of the hour. . . .

The world's greatest sea disaster darkened the early days of 1912. The Titanic, the greatest vessel afloat, the pride of Britain, the wonder of all nations, crashed its 46,000 tons on its maiden voyage against an ice-berg and sank in the sinister darkness. Of 2,224 souls on board only 707 were saved.

" Ragtime " had just arrived from America to startle the musical circles, and Pavlova's dancing was winning all hearts.

And then 1913. A year of anxiety, of foreboding, of unrest, and yet a year of high endeavour. On land and sea and in the air man's conquest continued. Buses and taxis and private motor-cars sprang from everywhere. An intrepid French aviator—Pegoud—looped the loop for the first time. Again the " writing in the sky ".

The militant Suffragettes clamoured for the vote. In their wild enthusiasm they flouted law and order and challenged society. They scaled the Monument in London to hang their flags and banners from the gilded crown of fire at the summit. On Derby Day, at Epsom, a Militant Suffragette hurled herself at Amner, the King's horse, bringing it down with the loss of her own life. " Votes for Women ! " was not to come yet.

Captain Scott led a second expedition to the South Pole, only to discover that he had been forestalled by Amundsen, the Norwegian. It was on this momentous expedition that Captain Oates, his injuries hampering the safe progress of his comrades, walked out to his death in the blizzard, " a very gallant gentleman."

Charlie Chaplin swam into the film firmament to dazzle the world with his clowning . . . one last, big laugh before the terror of '14.

That fateful year found Britain gay but apprehensive. Europe was a powder magazine. Even the friendly visit of the British Fleet to Kiel could not disguise the menace of the armaments race.

Women, however, still held the stage for a few fleeting months before the men were to march, Pagliacci-like, singing to their doom. Mrs. Buller was the first of her sex to fly professionally, and the Suffragettes, led by Mrs. Pankhurst, continued their battle, were arrested, imprisoned, went on hunger-strike, chained themselves to the gallery of the House and even attempted to petition the King.

Ascot fashions were a blaze of style and colour. A grim uncanny contrast to the waves of khaki that were so soon to enshroud the whole life of the nation.

And then, like a bolt from the clear, blue August sky, the Great War—the world butchery, the complete betrayal of sanity and reason.

The war pictures that are so important a section of this work have been chosen, not to make you shudder, but to make you *think*, to remember, to reflect, to realise, to resolve, " Never again."

Those who served will march once more with the invisible battalions of t]
who perished. Those who lost loved ones will speak a prayer that others may
suffer so. Those who do not remember, who are young and gay and free, a
young men were in 1914, will see why war, stripped of sudden change and glan
is sordid and shameful. The pity of it all ! The flower of a nation's man.
planted on foreign soil to wither and die. It is a queer, distorted thing this nobility
of battle. There is emotion, of course, in all the flags and bands and cheers, the
marching songs, the glint of sunlight on cold steel bayonets, the majesty of
trundling guns, 'planes waking the echoes in the heavens and the grey monsters of
the Fleet stealing stealthily from harbour to dawn. But what price glory when
you see the terrible reality? The squalor and misery ! The waste, the futility;
the sin of it. The hell of shot and shell fire, the fiendish cruelty of poison gas,
disease and every penalty of armed force. There are aspects of war you will not
see. But you will imagine them. Those who know will tell.

And then the Armistice. It has left us a legacy that endures through the years,
the Two Minutes' Silence in which the humblest and greatest in the land remember
those who lie " in some far corner of a foreign field " and resolve that generations
to come shall be saved from a second Armageddon.

There was the Victory March through London.

The Unknown Warrior was laid to rest in the Abbey.

But those post-war years had their mead of misery and danger. Not so easily
could the sins of war be wiped away. Strikes and the Slump, poverty and unemployment, problems of Empire. They arose to be faced by a war-tired people.
Many of them face us still.

Alcock and Brown conquered the Atlantic. They were the first to blaze the
air trail across the North Atlantic. British airmen have, since the war, held in their
hands the speed records of land and sea and air. The spirit of the old adventurers
still lives !

The launching of the *Queen Mary* was symbolic of our continued courage and
enterprise on the merchant routes. The openings of the Mersey Tunnel, the Sydney
Harbour Bridge, the growth of mighty buildings and highways proved that British
brains and workmanship are in the van of progress.

A Labour Government has been twice in office. The Trades Unions have
accomplished much with their programmes of sane and steady reform.

As you turn the pages that follow you will see an early crystal set through which,
over the ether, came sensational voices from 2LO. Science had discovered a
new world ! You will see the funeral of Queen Alexandra—loved by the people;
Gertrude Ederle, the first woman to swim the English Channel; the Graf " Zep "
sailing over London on its mission of peace, the Dartmoor Prison Mutiny, the Hatry
crash in the City; the Prince of Wales, spanning the world as the Ambassador of
Empire; the King, recuperating at the seaside after his critical illness; three Royal
weddings—all these are here and more.

History is perpetuated. The domestic, the national, the trend of thought
and things at home and abroad. This is a book of the past that will never be
closed. In it is the lesson of the future. Step by step in these pages you can
trace all the romance and adventure, the disappointments and disillusionments, the
courage and achievements of these twenty-five eventful years that have carried us
from Peace to War and from War to Peace. There are moments for rejoicing and
moments for reflection.

. " The Moving Finger writes and having writ, moves on. . . . . . "

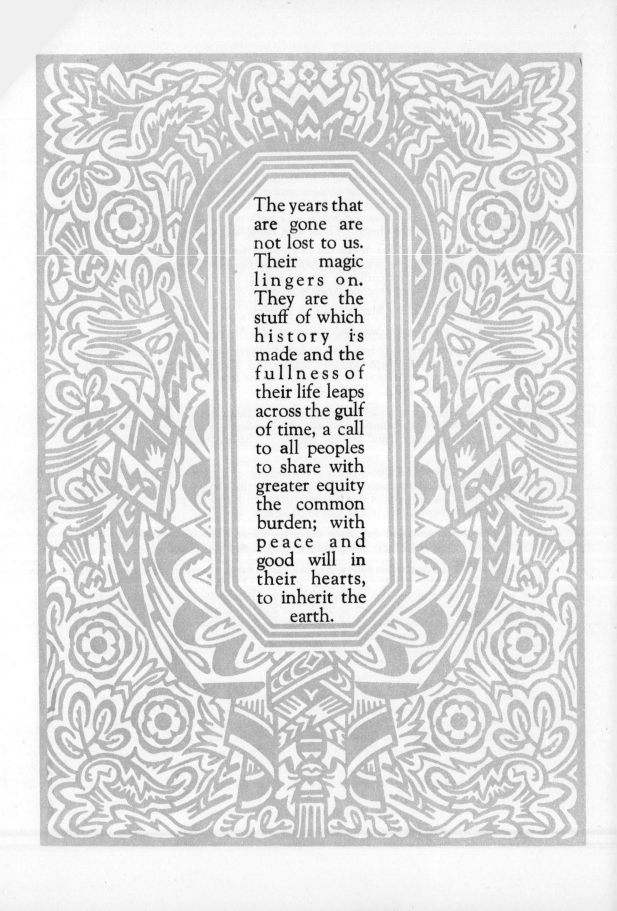

The years that
are gone are
not lost to us.
Their magic
lingers on.
They are the
stuff of which
history is
made and the
fullness of
their life leaps
across the gulf
of time, a call
to all peoples
to share with
greater equity
the common
burden; with
peace and
good will in
their hearts,
to inherit the
earth.

THE ACCESSION OF KING GEORGE V

13

Photo : Topical

On May 6, 1910, Edward VII died, and his son succeeded him as King George V. This photograph was taken on board the Royal yacht shortly before Edward the Peacemaker passed on to his son the heavy responsibilities of a King.

Three awed and solemn spectators in the garden of Marlborough House watched the scene in the Courtyard of St. James's Palace as the proclamation of the accession of George V was read to the assembled crowd on the morning of May 9— Prince Edward, right (who had become Duke of Cornwall), Prince Albert, left, and, in between them, Prince George.

Photos : S. and G., and Topical

And on May 20 the impressive funeral procession of the late King Edward VII passed through the streets, that were lined with his mourning subjects, on its way to Windsor, where he was finally laid to rest in the Chapel Royal.

1910

Photo : Topical

Two scenes in the funeral procession of King Edward VII are remembered as vivid and impressive incidents: King George V, the chief mourner, riding by the side of the Kaiser, who is carrying a Field-Marshal's baton, and the late King's

Photo : Topical

favourite charger, with boots reversed in the stirrups, led at a walking pace. The horse was followed by King Edward's dog, Caesar, who bore on his collar the inscription: "I am Caesar and I belong to Caesar."

17

Photo : Courtesy Austin Motor Co.

The 1910 Austin Car "Ascot" model priced at £420. It was a fifteen horsepower car and the hood, screen, windsheets, and headlights were "extras." Motor cars have certainly "gone a long way" since the year 1910!

Photo : Central Press

Shipbuilding was a great and prosperous industry and the nation was justly proud of the "luxury liners" which were beginning to be launched. This gymnasium aboard ship was considered very exciting and the very latest development of the changing ideas of health and exercise. These two are enjoying riding "mechanical horses."

Eros, the famous landmark of Piccadilly Circus, has seen some startling changes. The then fashionably dressed crowd strolling unconcernedly amid the slow horse-drawn traffic is a very different scene from that of to-day, when the ceaseless line of 'buses and cars makes crossing here a very risky undertaking except by the subways.

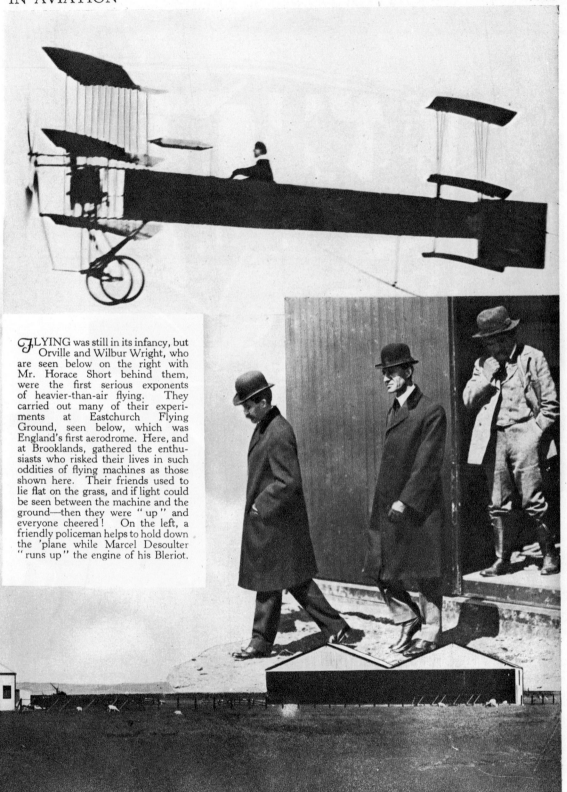

FLYING was still in its infancy, but Orville and Wilbur Wright, who are seen below on the right with Mr. Horace Short behind them, were the first serious exponents of heavier-than-air flying. They carried out many of their experiments at Eastchurch Flying Ground, seen below, which was England's first aerodrome. Here, and at Brooklands, gathered the enthusiasts who risked their lives in such oddities of flying machines as those shown here. Their friends used to lie flat on the grass, and if light could be seen between the machine and the ground—then they were " up " and everyone cheered ! On the left, a friendly policeman helps to hold down the 'plane while Marcel Desoulter " runs up " the engine of his Bleriot.

Photos : Flight

MR. ASQUITH (above) was
Prime Minister. Among
his problems were the many trade
disputes and strikes which followed
the depression of the past few years.

MR. JOSEPH CHAMBERLAIN
(right)—advocate of Tariff
Reform—was one of the most
popular men of his day. He was,
of course, the father of two sons
who figure prominently in politics
to-day, Mr. Neville Chamberlain
and Mr. Austen Chamberlain.

Photos : Topical

Photo : Topical

Mr. Lloyd George, seen here with his wife on the way to a Levee in 1910, was responsible for the National Health and Unemployment Insurance Scheme which created such excitement at this time. With " Ninepence for fourpence " as his slogan, he successfully piloted through the epoch-making Bill on which the Unemployment Scheme of to-day is based.

Mr. and Mrs. George Lansbury in 1910.

Photo : Topical

Photos : *Topical*

THE Labour Party was in its
infancy as far as its representation in the House of Commons; but
some of its members of those days
who have been prominent in recent
years were active then.   On the left,
Mr. George Lansbury, with his
wife;   above,   Mr. Ramsay Mac-
Donald;   and below, Mr. Henderson,
addressing a meeting in Ireland.

PRINCIPAL EVENTS OF 1910

JAN. 7. Mr. Latham broke aviation record for altitude by exceeding 3,000 ft.

,, 15. Polling General Election.

FEB. 1. First Labour Exchanges opened.

,, 15. New Parliament opened.

,, 16. Madame Curie succeeded in isolating one-tenth of a milligramme of polonium—possessing greater radio activity than radium.

,, 23. Dalai Lama and several noted Tibetans fled from Lhasa to India.

,, 25. First sitting of the Royal Commission on divorce.

,, 28. Last Chinese labourers left the Rand for China, ending employment of Chinese labour in South Africa.

MAR. 15. Foundations of National Association for Poor Law Reform.

,, 23. Eruption of Mount Etna.

,, 28. Boat Race won by Oxford.

APR. 21. Mark Twain dies.

,, 24. Marconi Transatlantic Wireless Service inaugurated.

,, 27. M. Paulham flew from London to Lichfield in a Farman aeroplane.

,, 28. M. Paulham reached Manchester, thus winning the *Daily Mail* Prize of £10,000 for first flight from London-Manchester.

MAY 6. Death of Edward VII.

,, 7. Oath of Allegiance to George V taken by Parliament. King George holds his first Privy Council.

,, 9. George V proclaimed King.

,, 17-19. Lying-in-State of King Edward.

,, 19. Earth passed through tail of Halley's Comet.

,, 20 Funeral of Edward VII.

JUNE 1. Derby Day. Lemberg won.

,, 2. Mr. C. S. Rolls flew from Dover to Calais and returned without landing on French soil. Time 90 minutes.

JUNE 23. Duke of Cornwall created Prince of Wales and Earl of Chester.

,, 28. Catholic Cathedral at Westminster consecrated.

JULY 1. *Terra Nova* leaves for the South Pole.

,, 31. Crippen and Ethel le Neve arrested.

AUG. 11. Altitude record broken by Mr. Drexel in Bleriot monoplane. 6,750 ft.

,, 13. Florence Nightingale died, aged 90.

SEPT. 7. Death of William Holman Hunt.

,, 22. Wireless between Ireland and Canada.

OCT. 3. Revolution in Portugal, Republic proclaimed, King Manoel and his mother leave for England.

,, 17. Gordon Bennett Balloon race started from St. Louis in America and landed on October 19 near Peribanku river. A record of 1,400 miles.

,, 18. Charing Cross Bank suspends payment.

,, 20. *Olympic* launched.

,, 22. Crippen found guilty.

,, 29. Mr. Graham-White wins the Gordon-Bennett International speed race of 100 kilo. 62½ m. in 1 hr. 4 mins. 3 secs.

NOV. 4. Duke of Connaught opens first parliament of The Union of South Africa.

,, 7. Opening of new General Post Office building, King Edward Street, E.C.

,, 11-15. Run on Birkbeck Bank.

,, 20. Tolstoi died, aged 82.

,, 22. Mr. Churchill horse-whipped by suffragette.

DEC. 2-20. General Election.

,, 10. *Mauretania* sailed to and from New York in 12 days.

,, 13. Mrs. Andrew Carnegie gives £2,000,000 to cause of peace.

,, 18. Mr. Tom Sopwith wins £4,000 aviation prize, flying from Eastchurch, Sheppy, to Beaumont, Belgium, 177 miles, in 3½ hours.

THE CORONATION OF KING GEORGE V

SIDNEY Street in Houndsditch was the scene, on January 3, of a pitched battle by police and troops with an armed gang led by a Russian desperado, Jacob Peters, alias "Peter the Painter." The criminals had barricaded themselves in one of the houses and maintained a fusillade of shots for nearly seven hours. Winston Churchill, then Home Secretary, arrived early on the scene and on his instructions a detachment of Scots Guards and a field gun were brought to the spot. He is shown on the opposite page watching the firing. This amazing episode was brought to a close unexpectedly by the intentional or accidental firing of the house. Some of the firemen were injured, and one is shown being lifted into an ambulance. The charred remains of the criminals were never identified.

Photos : Daily Mirror, and Topical

An extraordinary picture showing Mr. Winston Churchill,
then Home Secretary, at the famous "Siege of Sidney Street."

Photo : Central Press

Left : An exciting finish to the Egg-and-Spoon Race at a Sports meeting.

𝒯HE emancipation of women made very definite progress at this period. Preconceived ideas as to women's limitations went by the board. Athletics, cricket, golf—strenuous activities hitherto monopolised by men—were energetically taken up by women. Even the realm of aviation was invaded by such plucky pioneers as Mrs. Stocks, shown in the small photograph on the right-hand page. While in the larger picture below her is seen the correct attire of the day for playing golf !

Below : Vigorous cricket in progress in spite of hampering long skirts.

Photos : Daily Mirror

The
SPORTSWOMAN
of the
DAY

The pomp and pageantry of the Coronation procession surpassed anything hitherto seen in London. Whitehall

Photo : Haines

formed for the occasion and two days were given up to the procession to enable more people **to witness the spectacle.**

In the picture above the Peers are seen leaving the Abbey after the Coronation Service.

Photos : Topical

Here is the Coronation Coach passing along Whitehall. Every available window is crowded with sightseers.

Photo: S. and G.

Another view of the Coronation procession, passing through the Wellington Memorial Arch on Constitution Hill.

*C*HE "season" of 1911 easily surpassed in brilliancy all predecessors.
The magnet of the Coronation celebrations had attracted enormous crowds
from all parts of the country and from
abroad. The usual "fixtures" such
as the Lawn Tennis Championships
(then played in the old Worple Road
Courts at Wimbledon), Ascot and Cowes,
were all "packed to capacity." On the
left is Mrs. Lambert Chambers,
the Tennis champion of that year.

Below is a view of the Royal carriage
arriving on the racecourse at Ascot.

Photos: Topical

As a grand finale to the Cowes Regatta and the end of the season, His Majesty the King reviewed the Fleet at Spithead.

In the picture below may be seen during the Naval Review, the *Neptune*, then the largest British Dreadnought

Photos: S. and G.

EARLY
DAYS
in the
FILM
INDUSTRY

Photo: Will Day

The film industry was already making good headway in America, and below is a scene from one of Mary Pickford's early films which was then being shown. In Britain things were not so advanced. Above is R. W. Paul's first studio which was established at New Southgate. It could, in those days, be hired for a guinea a day. Comparatively little advance was made between 1910 to 1914, when films began really to boom.

PIONEERS IN MOVIE AND SOUND PICTURES

Above is a " still " from a British film made near Brighton. The actors were all local people. Despite the crudeness of British films, some pioneers of the industry were looking very far ahead. Below, Eugene Lauste may be seen already experimenting with " Talkies." In his back garden at Brixton he is taking the first combined movie and sound picture.

Photos: Will Day

During July the King's eldest son was presented to the people of Wales at Caernarvon Castle on the occasion of his investiture as Prince of Wales. It is an interesting point that in this year, the Red Dragon of Wales was revived in the coat

Photo: S. and G.   Drawings of the Arms prepared by the College of Arms

of arms of the Prince of Wales.   The left hand picture shows the coat of arms previous to 1911, with the arms of Saxe-Coburg carried on the shield.   The right-hand picture shows the arms as they are to-day, with the Dragon revived.

Photo : Topical

THE RAILWAY STRIKE of August 17-19 seriously paralysed transport throughout the country. Armed troops were called out to co-operate with the police in protecting vital points and to guard the people's food supplies. Above are food convoys leaving the docks under a strong escort of troops and police, and below a well-guarded Railway junction.

Photo : Topical

THE LAST HORSE BUS

OCTOBER 25 saw the last L.G.O.Co.'s horse vehicle making its final journey from London Bridge Station to Moorgate Street. The lower picture shows a typical daily scene in the omnibus stables.

Photos : L.P.T.B.

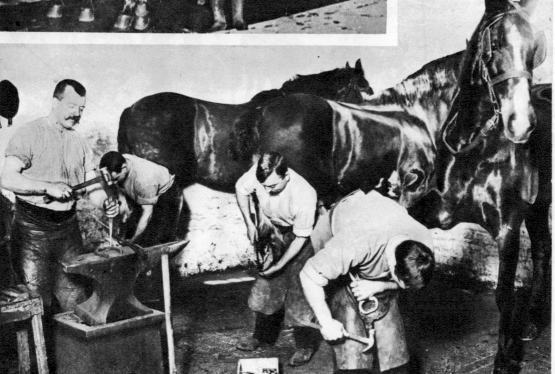

Photo : Topical

On August 27 at Hamburg the Kaiser made his sensational " Place in the Sun " speech, foreshadowing a big increase in the German Navy. This was interpreted in Britain as a challenge. The reply was to build more and more battleships, and

Photo : *Central Press*

on the left is seen the launch of the *King George V* at Portsmouth. Outwardly relations with Germany were still friendly. The King and the Kaiser paid each other periodic state visits. Above is a picture of them riding together in Berlin.

CHILDREN
of the
DAY

*C*HILDREN sprang a surprise on their elders by going on strike for less caning and more half-holidays. The youngsters took themselves quite seriously, but were soon back again at their desks after this juvenile attack of strike fever was cured. On the left is a scene on the banks of the Serpentine showing typical London children of the day. Below is a picture of a number of children from Elementary Schools in the Midlands.

Photo : Topical

Photo : Central Press

THE KING'S VISIT TO INDIA

On November 11 the King and Queen left England on board the *Medina* for the Delhi Durbar.

Photo : *Central Press* .

The splendour of the Delhi Durbar on December 12, surpassed anything that even India had ever seen. The picture above shows the King Emperor and his Royal Court in Coronation Robes beneath the blazing sun receiving the homage

Photo : S. and G.

of the Princes.   The photograph above is a more general view of the ceremony at the Royal Pavilion.   The event was the occasion for the announcement that henceforth Delhi was to be the capital of India in place of Calcutta.

PRINCIPAL EVENTS OF 1911

JAN. 1. Steinie Morrison arrested.
,, 3. Siege of Sidney Street.
,, 4. Australia wins second Test Match at Melbourne.
,, 10. Commander Sims of U.S. Navy reprimanded for stating that U.S.A. would help England if latter be threatened.

FEB. 4. Red Dragon of Wales to be revived in coat of arms of Prince of Wales.
,, 6. Ramsay Macdonald elected chairman of the Labour Party.

MAR. 10. Greenwich time became standard time of France.
,, 21. Tercentenary of authorised version of the Bible.
,, 24. Grand National won by Mr. F. Bibley's "Glenside."
,, 30. Launch of the super-Dreadnought *Monarch*.

APR. 1. Oxford and Cambridge Boat Race won by Oxford; time fastest on record— 18 minutes 29 seconds.
,, 2. Census.
,, 26. Cup-tie Final Replay—Bradford 1; Newcastle 0.

MAY 1. First "Labour Day" Demonstration. Inauguration of Folkestone-Flushing (night) mail route.
Penny Post to Australia inaugurated.
,, 2. English Sculling Championship won by Ernest Barry.
,, 6. Anniversary of death of Edward VII. Memorial service at Windsor.
,, 12. Display of military aviation at Hendon.
,, 16. Queen Victoria Memorial at Buckingham Palace unveiled by the King in presence of Kaiser and Kaiserin.
,, 23. Imperial Conference opened.
,, 27. King's birthday officially celebrated.
,, 29. Sir W. S. Gilbert dies, aged 74.
,, 31. *Titanic* launched.
Derby Day. Winner—Mr. J. B. Joel's "Sunstar."

JUNE 8. Suspension of Birkbeck Bank.
,, 10. The Prince of Wales created Knight of the Garter.
,, 17. 40,000 women demonstrated in favour of women's suffrage.
,, 22. Coronation of King George and Queen Mary.
,, 21. White Star Liner *Olympic*, largest ship afloat, completed her maiden voyage.

JULY 7-13 Royal visit to Ireland.
,, 13. Royal visit to Wales. Investiture of H.R.H. the Prince of Wales, at Caernarvon.
,, 29. World's Sculling championship won by Arnst.

AUG. 19. Great Rail Strike throughout United Kingdom terminated by a Conference at the Board of Trade.
,, 27. German Emperor's speech at Hamburg foreshadowing fresh increase of German Navy.

SEPT. 6. T. W. Burgess swims Channel.
,, 8. Mrs. Ramsay Macdonald dies aged 41.
,, 9. First Aerial Post in United Kingdom, Hendon to Windsor.
,, 13. Celebration 500 years St. Andrew's University.
,, 16. Jubilee of Post Office Savings Bank.

OCT. 4. Chinese Republic proclaimed.

NOV. 11. King and Queen leave for India.
,, 17. Crystal Palace sold
,, 26. French Government regulates air traffic.
,, 28. Mr. George Sanger ("Lord George Sanger"), circus proprietor, murdered.
,, 29. Meeting of female domestic servants at the Albert Hall to protest against their inclusion in the National Insurance Bill.

DEC. 2. King arrives at Bombay.
,, 12. Coronation Durbar at Delhi.
,, 14. Miss Eleanor Davies Colley, M.B. (Lond.), first woman to be admitted to the Royal College of Surgeons.

1912

RACE TO THE SOUTH POLE

Photo : Topical

"VOTES

PEACEABLE means had failed to win recognition for the cause of women's suffrage, and so, encouraged by Mrs. Pankhurst, the suffragettes resolved to try other means to bring themselves into the public eye. To get themselves arrested was their greatest aim. After an orgy of window-smashing in Regent Street (shown above.)

Photo : S. and G.

for WOMEN"

the suffragettes went cheerfully to Bow Street Police Station to answer to the charges made against them. The queue (shown above) waiting to hear the case shows that public interest had, indeed, been aroused. So eager were the window-smashers for prison, that they arrived complete with their luggage, and had to wait outside for the doors to open.

Photos : S. and G.

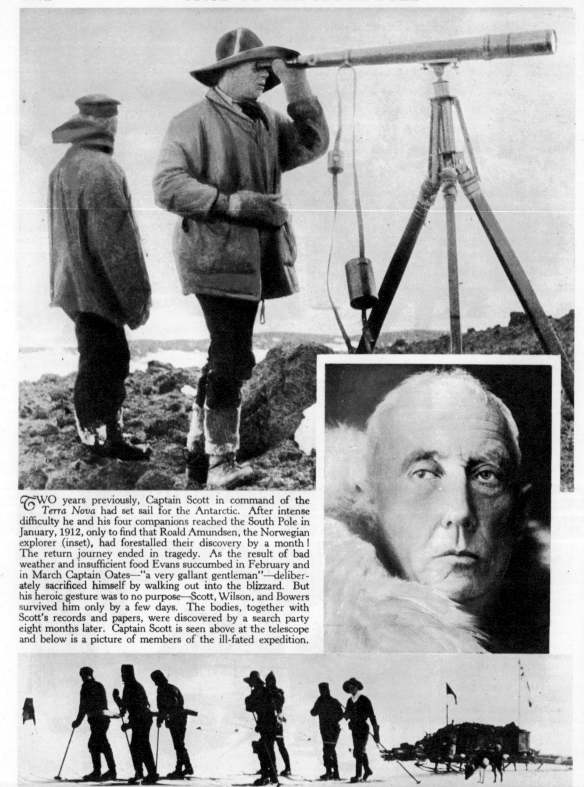

TWO years previously, Captain Scott in command of the *Terra Nova* had set sail for the Antarctic. After intense difficulty he and his four companions reached the South Pole in January, 1912, only to find that Roald Amundsen, the Norwegian explorer (inset), had forestalled their discovery by a month! The return journey ended in tragedy. As the result of bad weather and insufficient food Evans succumbed in February and in March Captain Oates—"a very gallant gentleman"—deliberately sacrificed himself by walking out into the blizzard. But his heroic gesture was to no purpose—Scott, Wilson, and Bowers survived him only by a few days. The bodies, together with Scott's records and papers, were discovered by a search party eight months later. Captain Scott is seen above at the telescope and below is a picture of members of the ill-fated expedition.

Photos : Topical

*C*HE marvel of wireless was just beginning to be generally accepted. Above is the Marconi station at Clifden, in Ireland, which had just been built. It was the first transatlantic wireless station in the British Isles. On the right is the powerful condenser then used, when experimenters in transmission thought that the greater the power used, the better the results would be.

On July 27, the extension of the London Tube Railway from the Bank to Liverpool St. was inaugurated. Below is the type of tube train then being built.

Photos : Marconi and L.P.T.B.

Photos: Topical and S. and G.

ON April 15 the ill-fated *Titanic* White Star liner struck an iceberg in fog and sank with the appalling loss of more than fifteen hundred lives out of a total of 2,224. Above is seen the liner being towed out on her maiden voyage; below, a number of the ship's boats which in the general panic that ensued were never used

THE
SINKING
of the
TITANIC

IN the picture on the right, the wireless operator is undergoing examination as to the time the S O S messages were sent out. And below is the crowd surrounding the White Star offices in a despairing effort to obtain the very latest news of the catastrophe.

Photos : S. and G.

Here is an informal snapshot of the Prince taken
as he went off for a morning round of golf.

Photo : S. & G.

To celebrate the fiftieth anniversary of her landing in England, Queen Alexandra inaugurated "Rose Day" on June 26. Above is seen the Queen Mother driving in London on that day, and below, one of the decorated cars. The sum raised for charity on the first Rose Day was £17,803.

Photos : Topical

Photo: *Topical*

On August 20, William Booth died, aged 83; first General of the Salvation Army that he had founded forty-seven years before.

Photo: S. & G.

The coffin of General Booth was followed to its last resting-place by huge crowds of saddened friends and workers.

Photo: Maycock, Odhams Press Ltd.

But he had started a movement that was to grow into the immense and powerful organisation as we know it to-day.

*T*HE sensational attack on Sir Edward Henry (seen on right) by a man to whom he had refused a taxi-driver's licence, brought him into prominence and reminded the public that he was responsible for the adoption by Scotland Yard of the finger-print system of criminal identification. The large picture shows part of the vast Scotland Yard index, that contains more than 250,000 finger-print entries.

Photo : Topical

WE WILL NOT HAVE HOME RULE FOR IRELAND.

Photo : Topical

The Irish question was prominent this year. Ireland herself was sharply divided on the question of Home Rule. Sir Edward Carson, who is seen above, was the powerful leader of the Ulstermen who did not want a separate Government.

FEB. 7. Centenary of Birth of Charles Dickens.

,, 10. Death of Lord Lister.

MAR. 7. Captain Amundsen and North Antarctic Expedition, having reached South Pole, arrive at Hobart from Buenos Aires.
M. Henrie Salmet flew London to Paris, non-stop, in 3 hours 25 min., in Bleriot monoplane.

,, 9. King lays foundation of New County Hall in London.

,, 10. Seddon convicted.

,, 26. King approved the title " The Royal Flying Corps."

,, 29. Loss of personnel of Scott Exp dition. Captain Scott, Dr. E. A. Wilson, Lieut. H. R. Bowers, Captain L. E. G. Oates (Mar. 1), Petty Officer E. Evans (Feb. 17).

,, 31. Home Rule Demonstration in Dublin, 100,000 present.

APR. 1. Captain Scott's ship *Terra Nova* arrived Akaroa, New Zealand, with news of Antarctic expedition.
Oxford won Boat Race.

,, 2. First woman passenger crosses channel by air with Hamel.

,, 8. New London Museum opened at Kensington.

,, 9. Great demonstration against Home Rule in Belfast.

,, 11. Introduction of Home Rule Bill.

,, 15. *Titanic* Disaster. W. T. Stead drowned.

,, 16. First appearance of the *Daily Herald.* Miss H. Quinley (U.S.A.) first woman pilot to cross Channel.

,, 24. Replayed Cup Tie Final—Barnsley 1; West Bromwich 0.

MAY 7. Centenary of Birth of Robert Browning.

,, 9. Tom Mann sentenced for inciting troops to mutiny.

,, 18. King and Queen opened new building of Royal Society of Medicine in Wimpole Street, London.

,, 22. Mr. and Mrs. Pethick Lawrence and Mrs. Pankhurst convicted of conspiracy and sentenced to nine months' imprisonment.

MAY 23. London Transport workers' strike.

,, 30. Wilbur Wright, pioneer aviator, dies, aged 45.

JUNE 5. Derby won by "Tagalie."

,, 17. Discovery of synthetic production of rubber on a commercial scale.

,, 24. Release from prison of Mrs. Pankhurst and Mrs. Pethick Lawrence owing to ill health.
Death of Sir George White, Defender of Ladysmith.

,, 26. First " Alexandra Rose Day " (£17,803 realised).

JULY 5. Cecil Rhodes' Memorial in Table Mountain dedicated by Lord Grey.

,, 15. National Insurance Act comes into force.

,, 27. London Tube Railway, Extension from Bank to Liverpool Street formally inaugurated.

,, 29. Ernest Barry (England) defeated Richard Arnst (New Zealand) in sculling championship of the world.

AUG. 7. At Dublin, Mrs. Mary Leigh and Miss Gladys Evans, Suffragists, got five years each for setting fire to Theatre Royal, Dublin, July 18. Mrs. Leigh released on licence, September 20, after 44 days' hunger strike.

,, 20. General Booth dies.

,, 21. Mr. Bramwell Booth succeeds as General of the Salvation Army.

OCT.14. Mr. Roosevelt shot at and wounded at Milwaukee.

,, 16. Turkey declares war on Bulgaria and Serbia.

,, 21. King signs declaration of neutrality.

NOV. 3. Turkish Appeal for mediation by the Powers.

,, 11-16. First International Motor Show, Olympia.

,, 16. Suffragettes who had walked from Edinburgh, presented petition to Prime Minister.

DEC. 3. Armistice agreed to in the Balkan War.

,, 7. Prince Louis of Battenberg became First Sea Lord of the Admiralty.
Renewal of Triple Alliance announced.

,, 16. Balkan Peace Conference.

,, 21. Delegates of Balkan States in Turkey to London Peace Conference, received by King.

MOTOR TRAFFIC BECOMES A PROBLEM

Photo : G.P.U.

The climax of the Suffragettes' efforts to obtain recognition occurred when Emily Davison, a prominent member of the movement, threw herself under the King's horse, Anmer, at the Derby. She died as a result of her injuries.

Photo : S. & G.

Another aspect of the great movement for the emancipation of women was the steady development of educational facilities for them. Here Her Majesty the Queen is seen opening the new wing of Bedford College, London University.

Photo : S. & G.

As evidence to the world of the amicable relations between the two countries, Monsieur Poincaré, the French President, paid an official visit to England in June. Above he is reviewing the guard of honour on his arrival.

Photo : "Flight"

Monsieur Pégoud, the French aviator, risked his life to substantiate Bleriot's theory of inverted flying. He is seen here taking off on his historic flight when he "looped the loop"—an evolution that is to-day quite commonplace.

Photo : Topical

Sir Thomas Lipton's *Shamrock III* was launched this year in preparation for the struggle between England and America for the America Cup. The race was to have taken place in 1914, but the outbreak of War cancelled all sports fixtures.

PRINCIPAL EVENTS OF 1913

JAN. 13. National Telephone Company taken over by the Post Office. Sum paid, £12,515,264.

,, 15. Medical benefit under Insurance Act begins.

,, 16. Third Reading, Home Rule Bill.

,, 17. M. Poincaré elected President of France.

,, 23. *Coup d'état* in Turkey; murder of Nazim Pasha.

,, 28. Opening by the Viceroy of first Legislative Council meeting at Delhi.

FEB. 10. Betrothal of Princess Victoria Louise, daughter of German Emperor, to Prince Ernst August.
News reaches London of deaths of Captain Scott and his companions in the Antarctic.

,, 14. International Aero Exhibition at Olympia.

,, 20. Great fire in Tokio.

,, 22. Death of Dowager Empress of China.

MAR. 4. Woodrow Wilson President U.S.A., Washington.

,, 13. Boat Race won by Oxford.

,, 18. Fall of Briand Ministry in France. Murder of King of Greece at Salonika.

,, 26. Death of Lord Wolseley, Field Marshal. Centenary of birth of David Livingstone.

,, 31. Death of John Pierpont Morgan, American banker.

APR. 2. Mrs. Pankhurst sentenced to three years' penal servitude.

,, 13. Attempt to assassinate King of Spain.

,, 19. Cup Tie Final at Crystal Palace : Aston Villa 1, Sunderland 0.

,, 21. Aquitania launched at Glasgow.

MAY 13. Agreement of the Balkan States to cease fighting and to send delegates to London for Conference.

,, 22. Centenary of Birth of Wagner.

,, 26. First appointment of woman magistrate (Miss Emily Duncan).

,, 30. Peace Treaty between Allies and Porte signed at St. James's Palace.

JUNE 2. Death of Alfred Austin, Poet Laureate.

,, 4. Suffragette, Miss Davison, fatally injured trying to stop King's horse at the Derby.

,, 9. Break up of Balkan Peace Conference.

,, 16-17. 25th Anniversary Kaiser's accession to throne.

,, 24-27. President Poincaré visits England.

JULY 1. New London-Paris service inaugurated via Dover-Calais.

,, 4. Queen opened new buildings of Bedford College for women in Regent's Park.

,, 10. Roumania declares war on Bulgaria.

,, 17. Dr. Robert Bridges appointed Poet Laureate.

,, 21. Centenary of Birmingham Chamber of Commerce.

,, 24. King and Queen lay foundation stone of new offices of Australian Commonwealth in the Strand.

,, 26. New building of King's College Hospital opened by King and Queen. Suffragist Pilgrimage meeting in Hyde Park.

AUG. 6. Peace Treaty signed by Bulgaria, Roumania, Greece, Serbia, and Montenegro at Bukharest.

,, 27. Palace of Peace opened at The Hague.

SEPT. 1. To test M. Bleriot's theories, the French airman Pégoud rose in a Bleriot machine 3,500 feet, turned it upside down, descended 1,500 feet in a *volplane*.

,, 4. Wedding of ex-King of Portugal and Princess Augusta of Hohenzollern.

,, 20. Second Aerial Derby won by Gustave Hamel.

,, 21. Serious rioting in Dublin.

,, 28. Peace signed between Bulgaria and Turkey.

OCT. 10. Panama Canal formally opened.

,, 15. Prince Arthur of Connaught marries Duchess of Fife.

,, 16. *Queen Elizabeth* launched (oil driven).

,, 30. Death of Dr. Rudolf Diesel—inventor of the Diesel engine.

NOV. 7. Box Hill, Surrey, presented to the nation.

,, 12. Accession of King Ludwig of Bavaria.

,, 13. Greco-Turkish treaty signed.

DEC. 8. Bombardier Wells knocked out by Carpentier in first round.

,, 9. At Montreal piercing was completed of the Canadian Northern Railway Tunnel under Mount Royal.

,, 12. " Mona Lisa," which had been stolen from the Louvre, recovered in Florence.

,, 17. Crystal Palace purchased for the nation.

,, 25. On Christmas Day no London newspaper appeared.

,, 30. Death of the Dowager Queen of Sweden.

THE DRUMS OF WAR

EVENTS in Europe were over-shadowed by the trouble in Ireland in 1914. The strife between the Ulster loyalists, headed by Sir Edward Carson, and the Home Rule Party resulted in a dangerous and critical situation. Mr. John Redmond (in top hat), leader of the Home Rule Party, is seen here leaving Buckingham Palace, after an audience with the King. Mr. Redmond assured the government on the outbreak of war that Ireland would be loyal to England.

Photo : Topical

DURING the earlier troubled months of 1914, Sir James Craig's house was guarded by troops when Sir Edward Carson, the leader of the Ulstermen, stayed there. On the left is seen the changing of the guard.

And on both sides volunteers practised first-aid anticipating actual hostilities, which indeed did take place in July.

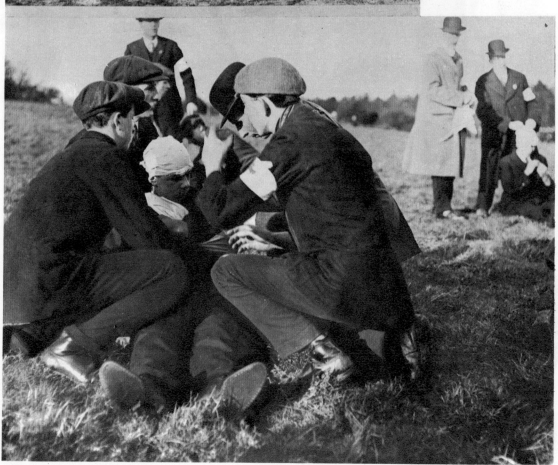

Photos : S. & G.

Photos : Topical

THE last great suffragette demonstration took place in the early months of 1914 when Mrs. Pankhurst and her supporters attempted to petition the King at Buckingham Palace. Mrs. Pankhurst was arrested for the eighth time in three years. She is seen above being carried off bodily by a policeman. On the left one of her followers refuses to get up, despite repeated attempts by the police to lift her.

On June 13 His Royal Highness the Prince of Wales performed his first public ceremony—laying the foundation stone of St. Anselm's Church, Kensington. The Prince, aged 20, was embarking on his public career.

Photo : S. & G.

SARAJEVO

ON June 26, 1914, occurred the tragedy in Sarajevo which eventually plunged all Europe into war. The Archduke Francis Ferdinand of Austria was assassinated by Prinzip, a Serbian. In her note of protest Austria made such heavy demands for compensation that Serbia refused to comply. Austria, supported by Germany, declared war. Russia joined in on the side of Serbia. France, the sworn ally of Russia, was immediately embroiled; and two days after, England declared war on Germany in accordance with her written obligation to uphold the neutrality of Belgium, which had been invaded by Germany. Above is a photograph of the Archduke Ferdinand and his wife, taken only a few minutes before their death, and on the left is shown the arrest of the assassin.   Inset, Prinzip.

Photos : Cossira

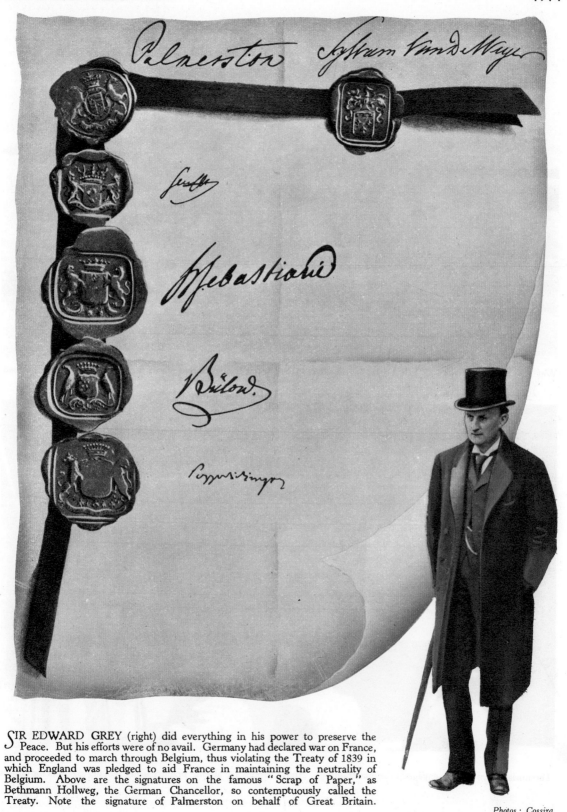

SIR EDWARD GREY (right) did everything in his power to preserve the
Peace. But his efforts were of no avail. Germany had declared war on France,
and proceeded to march through Belgium, thus violating the Treaty of 1839 in
which England was pledged to aid France in maintaining the neutrality of
Belgium. Above are the signatures on the famous "Scrap of Paper," as
Bethmann Hollweg, the German Chancellor, so contemptuously called the
Treaty. Note the signature of Palmerston on behalf of Great Britain.

Photos : Cossira

War was almost inevitable. The Fleet was recalled in full force from manœuvres at the annual review at Spithead.

Photo : Will Day

Territorials were actively engaged in annual training. Above, troops are at rifle practice using moving pictures for targets.

Photo : I.W.M.

It was generally realised by the nation that the Grand Fleet was assembled awaiting the outbreak of hostilities.

Photo : Topical

Above, the London Scottish, soon to be sent to the front, practising the charge with fixed bayonets.

Photo : Cen. Press

WILL IT BE WAR

THE August holiday crowds were as dense as ever. Above is seen a busy London Terminus Station, and on the left, a typical river scene. Despite rumours of war, few people realised how grave was the situation.

Photo : Topical

Photo : S. & G.

THE night of August 3rd was one that will never be forgotten. The streets of London were filled with people anxious to hear the latest news. A vast crowd assembled outside Buckingham Palace and greeted the King with loyal applause when he appeared before them on the balcony.

OR

PEACE ?

On the same day the Naval Reserves had been called up by Royal Proclamation— the appearance of this Proclamation (reproduced on the right) was an indication to the public of the gravity of the crisis.

BY THE KING.
A PROCLAMATION

For Calling out Men of the Royal Naval Reserve and Royal Fleet Reserve, and Officers and Men of the Royal Naval Volunteer Reserve.

GEORGE R.I.

WHEREAS by the fourth section of the Royal Naval Reserve (Volunteer) Act, 1859, it is enacted that it shall be lawful for Us on such occasions as We shall deem fit (the occasion being first communicated to Parliament if Parliament be sitting or declared in Council and notified by Proclamation if Parliament be not sitting or in being) to order and direct that the Volunteers under that Act, or so many or such part of them as We may deem necessary, shall be called into actual service:

And whereas by the Royal Naval Reserve Volunteer Act, 1896, as amended by the Royal Naval Reserve Act, 1902, it is enacted that the power under the said Act of 1859 to raise and pay Volunteers may be exercised outside the British Islands in respect of British subjects:

And whereas by the Naval Reserve Act, 1900, the Admiralty are authorized to raise and keep up a new division, commonly known as the Royal Fleet Reserve, of the force raised under the said first recited Act in addition to the men raised under that Act, and such new division is liable to be called out as part of the Royal Naval Reserve under the said fourth section of the said Act of 1859:

And whereas by the Naval Forces Act, 1903, it is provided that the Admiralty may raise and maintain a force to be called the Royal Naval Volunteer Reserve, and that certain provisions of the said Act of 1859 (including the fourth section of that Act) as amended by any subsequent enactment shall apply to the force so raised:

And whereas by the first section of the Naval Reserve (Mobilisation) Act, 1900, amending the said Act of 1859, it is enacted that it shall be lawful for Us where We order and direct that Volunteers under that Act shall be called into actual service to authorize the Admiralty to give and, when given, to revoke or vary such directions as may seem necessary or proper for calling out all or any of the said Volunteers as the occasion may require:

And whereas Parliament is not sitting:

And whereas We have declared in Council and hereby notify that owing to the state of Public Affairs and the demands upon Our Naval Forces for the protection of the Empire an occasion has arisen for ordering and directing as in the said Act provided:

WE DO by this Our Proclamation order and direct that Volunteers under the said Acts shall be called into actual service:

AND WE do hereby authorize the said Lords Commissioners of the Admiralty to give and, when given, to revoke or vary such directions as may seem necessary or proper for calling out all or any of the said Volunteers as the occasion may require.

Given at Our Court at Buckingham Palace, this Third day of August, in the year of our Lord one thousand nine hundred and fourteen, and in the Fifth year of Our Reign.

GOD SAVE THE KING.

Photo : I.W.M.

Photo : Topical

Photo : S. & G.

WAR

IS

DECLARED

AUGUST 4. War is declared ! Recruits in great numbers to serve in the forces were immediately forthcoming. Whitehall (left) was thronged with teeming multitudes anxious to read the official Declaration of War. Above is shown a procession of would-be soldiers marching through Hyde Park, and (right) one of the first of many recruiting posters issued.

RALLY ROUND
THE FLAG
EVERY
FIT MAN
WANTED

Photo : I.W.M.

The Fleet was under the command of Admiral Jellicoe, seen here aboard H.M.S. *Iron Duke*.

Photo : I.W.M.

THE FLEET IS READY

IMMEDIATELY on the outbreak of war the Fleet received orders to move to its battle stations. Owing to the initiative of the Admiralty, the British Navy was ready and waiting when the call came to act as "Britain's Sure Shield." Above is shown a section of the Grand Fleet "full steam ahead," and on the right a typical scene in the stokehold.

Photos : I.W.M.

Photo : S. & G.

THE
CALL
to
ARMS

RECRUITING continued
briskly. Public figures lent
themselves to the task of arousing
popular enthusiasm. On the left
is George Robey addressing a
large crowd in Trafalgar Square.
And above, a recruiting sergeant
gives instructions through a
megaphone to the " raw material"
who have just enlisted, before
they leave for training centres.

From the Film, " The Soul of a Nation"

(*Above*). The Public Schools Brigade left for camp in a fleet of omnibuses. War was then for them an exciting adventure. Only when it came to saying good-bye as the troop-train drew out did the grim reality that this might be a final parting loom large. Many left behind comforted themselves by saying the war would finish in six months.

Photos: S. & G.

Photo : Cossira

Sir John French was in charge of the first British Expeditionary Force.   He is seen arriving at Boulogne.

Photo: " Flight "

The possibilities of the Royal Flying Corps, which had come into existence only two years before, had not yet been fully realised. It was thought that it " might be useful for observation." Here is a line-up of 'planes that went into action in 1914.

Photo: I.W.M.

The first British Expeditionary Force enjoyed a wonderful reception at each station on its way through France to the front.

An ingeniously-arranged ambush is here seen occupied by a German machine-gun detachment during the invasion of Belgium. The ambush was cleverly used by the Germans where fighting was confined to isolated units on each side.

Belgium was now being occupied and suffered all the humiliations of enemy invasion, resisting, staunchly, to the last. The Germans systematically searched and interrogated the civilians, lest they should be carrying concealed arms.

Photos : Cossira

The scene of a halt by the wayside was common. All over Belgium vast hordes of field-grey uniforms swept like an all-engulfing flood, while hosts of homeless refugees, having evacuated their homes, sought safety over the frontier.

An extraordinary picture of the German army in their uniforms of field grey
and their spiked helmets, advancing in endless waves through the fields during

:heir onward sweep across Belgium. One town after another, including
many great fortresses, fell before the overwhelming masses of enemy troops.

FIRST
BATTLE of
the MARNE

*T*HE Battle of the Marne began on September 6. As yet, fighting was still, for the most part, in the open. On the left a shell has just exploded on the roadside while supplies of ammunition are being rushed to the guns at the Front. After that first terrible autumn retreat from Mons, the enormous casualty lists which appeared daily in the Press, was a grim indication of the destructive power of modern warfare. The picture below shows crowds watching ambulances carrying wounded from the front into Charing Cross Hospital.

Photo : I.W.M.

Photo : I.W.M.

Photo : S. & G.

Every possible form of transport was utilised to carry troops to the front. London buses filled with troops became a common sight on French country roads.   Here are Scottish troops being rushed to the front line.

Photo : I.W.M.

Photo : S. & G.

In the winter of 1914, Scarborough was bombarded from the sea, with much damage to property—a foretaste of the subsequent raids on our shores by enemy warships and aircraft. Above is seen a house wrecked by enemy shell fire.

LORD KITCHENER
TAKES CHARGE

AN outstanding figure of 1914-15 was Lord Kitchener, who as soon as the extent of the crisis was realised was dramatically recalled after he had departed for the East, and was immediately appointed Secretary of State for War. Largely by his efforts and his prestige were raised Kitchener's Armies, which played such a decisive part in the War.

THE photo below, shows the sinking of H.M.S. *Audacious*, one of the most sensational incidents of the early War. The news, carefully withheld from the British press, was circulated in America, from whence it filtered back across the Atlantic.

Photo : Cossira

Photo : I.W.M.

D

Photo : I.W.M.

Another epic of the sea was the battle off Cocos Islands between the famous German raider *Emden* and the Australian cruiser *Sydney*, resulting in the destruction of the enemy ship. The *Sydney's* boats are here seen rescuing the crew.

Photo : I.W.M.

On December 16 the news came to the fleet anchored in the Firth of Forth that enemy warships were on the way to raid our shores. That evening, as darkness fell, the great ships slipped quietly out of Rosyth Base "to keep the tryst."

PRINCIPAL EVENTS OF 1914

JAN. 21. Death of Lord Strathcona, High Commissioner for Canada, aged 93.

FEB. 25. Death of Sir John Tenniel. aged 93.

MAR. 4. Death of Earl of Minto, Gov.-Gen. of Canada 1898-1904, Viceroy of India 1905-1910. Aged 68.
,, 28. Boat Race won by Cambridge.
,, 30. Mr. Asquith, Prime Minister, assumes post as Minister for War.

APR. 5. Cup Tie Final, Burnley 1, Liverpool 0.
,, 17. Britannia Pier, Yarmouth, burned down by suffragettes.

MAY 21. Suffragist riot outside Buckingham Palace.
,, 23. Gustav Hamel drowned flying Channel.
,, 27. Derby Day. Mr. H. B. Duryea's Durbar won.

JUNE 8. First liner towed through Gatum Lock, Panama.
,, 11. Bomb outrage in Edward the Confessor's Chapel, Westminster Abbey, by suffragettes.
,, 22. Kitchener created an Earl in King's Birthday Honours.
,, 26. King and Queen opened King George's Dock at Hull.
,, 28. Assassination of Archduke Francis Ferdinand of Austria and his wife at Sarajevo.

JULY 2. Death of Mr. Joseph Chamberlain.
,, 16. Georges Carpentier defeated " Gunboat " Smith (America).
,, 21. Shah of Persia crowned at Teheran.
,, 28. Austria-Hungary declares war on Serbia.
,, 30. Belgrade taken by Austrians. Russia begins to mobilise.
,, 31. London Stock Exchange closed. Bank rate raised to 8 per cent.

AUG. 1. The *Endurance*, with Sir E. Shackleton's Antarctic Expedition leaves for South Polar regions.
Germany declares war on Russia and France.
,, 2. German invasion of France. Russian troops cross East Prussian frontier. Admiralty call out Naval reserves. Partial Moratorium decreed in the United Kingdom.
,, 3. German Ultimatum to Belgium. British Fleet mobilised.

Aug. 4. German invasion of Belgium.
British Ultimatum to Germany.
War Declared.
Sir John Jellicoe assumes command of Grand Fleet in North Sea.
Sir John French appointed to command Expeditionary Force.
,, 5. Earl Kitchener of Khartoum appointed Secretary for War.
Issue of Treasury notes for 10s. and £1.
,, 8. British Expeditionary Force lands in France.
,, 10. Liege occupied by Germans.
France declares war on Austria-Hungary.
,, 12. Defence of the Realm Act passed.
,, 12. Great Britain declares war on Austria-Hungary.
,, 15. Panama Canal formally opened.
,, 20. Pope Pius X dies; Cardinal della Chiesa succeeds as Benedict XV.
German occupation of Brussels.
,, 24. Fall of Namur.
,, 26. Destruction of Louvain.
,, 31. Arrival of the Queen of Belgians and her children at Dover.

SEPT. 1. St. Petersburg to be known as Petrograd.
,, 6. Battle of Marne begins.
,, 15. Battle of the Aisne begins.
,, 24. Trench warfare begins.

OCT. 9. Fall of Antwerp.
,, 10. Death of King of Roumania.
,, 14. First Canadian troops arrive at Plymouth.
,, 29. Turkey enters the War.
Lord Fisher appointed First Sea Lord.

NOV. 5. Military execution of Karl Lody in Tower for espionage.
,, 5. Great Britain declares war on Turkey.
,, 14. Death of Earl Roberts at St. Omer.
,, 17. Issue of £350,000,000 War Loan.
,, 23. British squadron bombarded Zeebrugge.

DEC. 4. The King visits the Front in France.
,, 8. Battle of the Falkland Islands.
,, 16. German bombardment of Hartlepool, Scarborough and Whitby
,, 17. Egypt proclaimed British Protectorate.
,, 24. Air Raid on Dover.
,, 25. Informal Christmas truce – hostilities resumed at midnight.

Photo : I.W.M.

MORE RECRUITS WANTED

Photos : I.W.M. and Cossira

Under the command of Rear-Admiral the Hon. H. L. A. Hood (inset) the Dover Patrol came into being. It consisted at first of ordinary fishing trawlers, manned generally by their own crew, though later other craft were added. The all-important business of the Patrol throughout the War was to keep the English Channel free from mines and submarines.

All round the coast fishermen who knew the home waters intimately were invaluable in assisting the mine-sweepers in their dangerous work. Two " old salts " of Harwich are here seen discussing the new " catches " they are sent out to make. Women, too, helped in the task of keeping the Channel free. While the men were at sea, they did their little bit ashore.

Photos : I.W.M.

On January 24 a battle was fought in the North Sea between the German battle-cruisers *Seydlitz*, *Derfflinger*, *Moltke*, and *Blücher*, supported by light cruisers and destroyers, and British ships among which were H.M.S. *Lion* (commanded by Vice-Admiral Sir David Beatty), *Tiger*, *Princess Royal*, *New Zealand*, and *Indomitable*. The *Blücher* was so damaged

Photo : Daily Mail

that she capsized and sank.   This remarkable photograph was taken as she heeled over, just before the final plunge.
Less than 200 of a total complement of nearly 1,000 were saved.   The picture clearly shows the men scrambling over
the sides of the ship, while clouds of smoke and steam belch forth as the sea pours down the funnels on to the furnaces.

Photo : I.W.M.

In France the combatants had gone to ground.   The war on land would henceforward be fought from trenches.   Here
is a Guardsman in his sheepskin winter coat and woollen Balaklava helmet standing amid the icy slush of the first snows.

The 21st Infantry Brigade (7th Division) had their headquarters in a haystack during the battle of Neuve Chappelle!

Photos : I.W.M.

A view of the 2nd Suffolks entrenched in Bellyache Wood near Spoilbank and the Ypres-Comines canal. The wood derived its name from a spring of water with medicinal properties whose unpleasant reputation was widely known.

In the early months of 1915, a new and terrible form of warfare was introduced by the Germans. This was liquid fire. Above, soldiers are watching a demonstration, and learning how to handle this new form of weapon.

Photos : I.W.M.

This photograph shows the terrifying flame-throwing apparatus actually in use by the Germans during an attack.

Then on April 22 in a violent assault on the Allied positions in front of Ypres, gas was introduced for the first time. Above is seen one of the earliest patterns of gas-masks, pads of cotton-wool soaked in a solution of common washing-soda.

Photos : I.W.M.

The above picture shows German naval troops wearing early types of respirator, in preparation for an expected gas attack.

In May a disaster occurred at Gretna Green, when a train crowded with troops was involved in a terrible collision—157 people were killed and 200 injured. The photograph taken shortly after the accident shows a small part of the wreckage.

Photos · S. & G.

On May 7, the *Lusitania* was torpedoed by a German submarine off the south of Ireland; 1,198 persons lost their lives. The picture shows only a small portion of the anxious crowds that gathered outside the Cunard Offices in London.

On June 23 His Royal Highness the Prince of Wales attained his twenty-first birthday. He was then serving with the forces.

1915

112

LANDING AT GALLIPOLI

THIS picture, reproduced from a famous painting (by Cyrus Cuneo), represents the landing on April 25, at Anzac—a cove on the coast of Gallipoli, near Gaba Tepe. The Australian and New Zealand troops had to make their way up a steep incline, completely exposed to the murderous fire of the Turkish guns on the heights above. The word Anzac was used to denote Australian and New Zealand troops who served in the War, and was derived from the initial letters of the Australian and New Zealand Army Corps. The cove got its name from the incident illustrated.

Above: the form of ferry used to carry our troops across the Bay.   Below: the store dumps fired before evacuation

Photos: I.W.M.

The campaign in Gallipoli, " The Glorious Failure," was an attempt to wrest the control of the Dardanelles from the Turks.   British, Australian, and New Zealand and French Colonial troops were landed on the exposed shores, but despite all the heroic efforts and grim determination of the men, it was realised that evacuation was the only possible solution.

Above : British soldiers digging trenches on an exposed hillside in the blazing sun.   Below : an Anzac's farewell to Gallipoli.

Photos : I.W.M.

The authorities decided that the position could not be held. Evacuation began in December and ended in January, 1916.   The cost of the terrible expedition was over 31,000 killed, 78,000 wounded, and 9,500 were missing.   The evacuation itself was a triumph of organisation and was carried out practically without any loss of life.

Photo : I.W.M.

THE power of the written and pictured appeal was never more strongly evidenced than by these war posters of 1915. They were, of course, used for the recruiting of troops for Lord Kitchener's New Armies.

Photos : I.W.M.

Photo : Cossira

Many unusual forms of transport were pressed into service during the war but surely none more odd than this circus elephant commandeered by German troops in the occupied areas, for hauling timber to be used for trench props.

Photo : I.W.M.

Zeppelins were beginning to prove ineffectual against the attacks of aeroplanes and anti-aircraft guns, although they continued to raid our shores until well on in 1917. Here is an aerial view of a Zeppelin brought down in the Channel in August by the Dover Anti-Aircraft guns, where it was bombed on the water by the R.N.A.S. pilots from Dunkirk. It is being towed back to Ostend where it was eventually broken up and its remains transported by rail to Germany.

Photo: Topical

Nurse Cavell, Matron of the Berkendael Medical Institute, Brussels, has become a national figure.   During the German occupation of Brussels she was accused of assisting soldiers to escape across the frontier to Holland.   Her trial by court-martial, took place on October 7, and in spite of efforts made by neutral powers to save her, she was shot five days later. Her remains are in Norwich Cathedral, and an impressive memorial is at the bottom of St. Martin's Lane, London.

PRINCIPAL EVENTS OF 1915

JAN. 19. Zeppelin bombs dropped on Yarmouth.

,, **25.** Canadian Northern Railway from Lake Superior—Pacific Coast completed.

,, **28.** Announcement of British loan of £5,000,000 to Roumania.

FEB. 2. Turks defeated on the Suez Canal.

,, **11.** British aeroplanes and seaplanes bombard Bruges and Ostend.

,, **18.** German blockade of Great Britain begins.

,, **19.** Bombardment of the Dardanelles begins.

,, **21.** German aeroplane raid on Essex.

MAR. 10. British take Neuve Chapelle.

,, **20.** Air raid on Deal.

,, **29.** Bombardier Wells knocked out by F. Moran (U.S.A.).

APR. 14. Zeppelin raid on the Tyneside.

,, **16.** Zeppelin raid on Lowestoft, Maldon, etc.

,, **18.** British take Hill 60. Death of Baron de Reuter, Managing Director, Reuter's Telegram Co., Ltd.

,, **23.** Rupert Brooke dies, aged 27.

,, **25.** Allied forces land at Gallipoli.

,, **30.** Zeppelin bombs on Ipswich and Bury St. Edmunds.

MAY 7. *Lusitania* torpedoed.

,, **10.** Zeppelin bombs on Southend.

,, **13.** German Princes and the Emperors of Germany and Austria struck off roll of Knights of the Garter.

,, **17.** Zeppelin raid on Ramsgate.

,, **19.** All racing suspended (except at Newmarket) for the duration of War.

,, **22.** Gretna Green troop train railway disaster.

,, **23.** Italy declares war on Austria.

,, **25.** Coalition Ministry announced by Mr. Asquith. Mr. Lloyd George : Minister of Munitions.

,, **26.** *Triumph* torpedoed.

,, **27.** Zeppelin raid on Southend.

,, **31.** Zeppelin raid on London.

JUNE 6. Zeppelin raid on East Coast.

,, **7.** Zeppelin destroyed by Lieut. Warneford, R.N.

,, **9.** Ministry of Munitions established.

,, **23.** His Royal Highness The Prince of Wales comes of age.

JULY 9. German South West Africa conquered.

,, **14.** National Registration Act passed.

AUG. 3. King presented first colours to Welsh Guards.

,, **4.** Tribitch Lincoln arrested.

,, **5.** Fall of Warsaw.

,, **10.** Air Raid on East Coast.

,, **13.** Another raid on East Coast.

,, **15.** National Register taken throughout Great Britain.

,, **19.** White Star liner *Arabic* torpedoed.

,, **20.** Italy declares war on Turkey.

SEPT. 4. The liner *Hesperian* torpedoed.

,, **7-13.** Zeppelin raids on East Coast.

,, **8.** Air Raid on London.

,, **19.** Bulgaria mobilises.

,, **25.** Beginning of Great Allied offensive on Western Front.

,, **26.** Death of Kier Hardie, M.P.

OCT. 5. Allied forces land at Salonika.

,, **11.** Lord Derby, new Director of Recruiting.

,, **12.** Nurse Cavell executed at Ghent.

,, **13.** Zeppelin raid on London and Eastern Counties.

,, **14.** Bulgarian armies attack Serbia.

,, **15.** Great Britain declares war on Bulgaria.

,, **16.** France declares war on Bulgaria.

,, **19.** Italy declares war on Bulgaria.

,, **23.** Dr. W. G. Grace dies.

DEC. 12. Lt.-Gen. Sir William Robertson appointed Chief of Imperial General Staff.

,, **15.** Sir Douglas Haig succeeds Sir John French in France.

,, **19.** Withdrawal begins from Anzac and Suvla Bay.

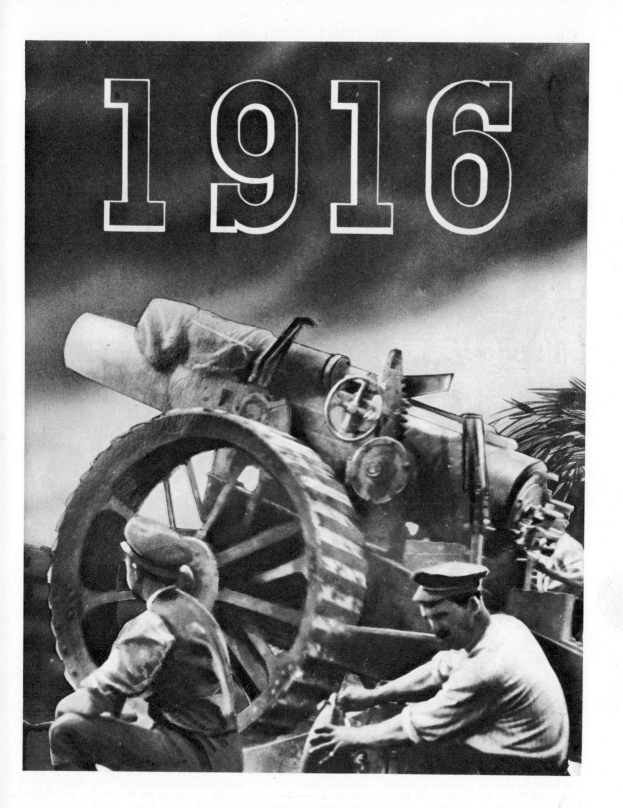

FEEDING THE GUNS!

Photo : Cossira & Topical

On Easter Sunday the "trouble in Ireland" came to a head and for a week open rebellion raged. The Sinn Fein—or Nationalist Party—chose this time to strive towards an independent Ireland. Much damage was done by fire and artillery. The picture shows the wreckage of barriers and burnt-out cars in a Dublin Square. Inset: Sir Roger Casement, ex-Consul at Rio de Janeiro, who was tried on May 15 on a charge of "adhering to the King's enemies," and enlisting German aid in the Sinn Fein cause. He was found guilty of treason, sentenced to death and hanged on August 3.

With no indication, as yet, that the end of the War was in sight, economy became more essential than ever. Any form of extravagance was discouraged, and, as the poster in the picture indicates, even over-dressing was regarded as disloyal.

Photos : I.W.M.

Among the numerous women's organisations the "Waacs" (Women's Army Auxiliary Corps) and the "Wrens" (Women's Royal Naval Reserve) were the most widely known. Here are some members of the latter corps at revolver practice.

Photos : I.W.M.

On May 31 and June 1 was fought the Battle of Jutland between the British and German fleets. Sir David Beatty, with a force of six battle-cruisers and four battleships, put out from Rosyth, and Sir John Jellicoe, with 24 battleships and 3 battle-cruisers, from Scapa Flow. Each was attended by destroyers, cruisers and other auxiliary craft. In the afternoon of the 31st the first encounter took place in which the *Indefatigable* and the *Queen Mary* were destroyed in the first half-hour. The *Tiger* and the *Lion* were also badly damaged, as were the *Lützow* and two other German ships. The top picture shows the *Queen Mary* exploding and, below, the German battle-cruiser *Seydlitz* in the thick of the combat belching smoke.

Photos : I.W.M.

The main German Fleet, under the command of Admiral von Scheer, now came up. The British Grand Fleet under the command of Admiral Sir John Jellicoe came down from the North West, and a second engagement took place during which H.M.S. *Invincible*, when close to the German battle-cruiser *Derfflinger*, was struck amidships by a 12-in. shell that ignited the magazines. The top picture was taken a fraction of a second before the explosion that broke the ship in half and killed 1,025 men out of a total of 1,031. The lower picture shows German shells bursting near the *Birmingham*.

Illustrated London News

This picture, drawn from details supplied by eye witnesses at the Battle of Jutland, shows H.M.S. *Shark* fighting gallantly even as the waves closed over her. Commander Loftus Jones remained in charge of the *Shark's* last gun although one of his legs had been shot away. Finally as the ship settled down under water, he gave orders for the last torpedo to be fired.

Photo : I.W.M.

As night came on, the British battleships drew off and prepared to renew the attack at dawn. When morning came however, it was found that the German fleet had escaped in the darkness to the shelter of its own minefields. The inset picture is a characteristic one of Vice-Admiral Beatty, who was in command of a section of the Fleet at Jutland. Here is a view of one of the damaged ships after the battle. The huge hole in its side is stuffed temporarily with bedding.

Photo : Daily Express

The death of Lord Kitchener, who went down in the H.M.S. *Hampshire* on June 5, 1916, was a severe shock to the nation. Here he is seen only a few hours before his death, on board the Flagship H.M.S. *Iron Duke*, at Scapa Flow. Beside him is Captain Sir Frederic Dreyer (Flag Captain of H.M.S. *Iron Duke*), and behind them are Admiral Jellicoe and Colonel FitzGerald, Kitchener's secretary. A few minutes after, Kitchener boarded the cruiser H.M.S. *Hampshire* for his last voyage.

Photo : I.W.M.

An impressive picture of a Battle Squadron of the Grand Fleet patrolling the North Sea, keeping their ever vigilant watch.

IN the early morning of July 1 began the great Battle of the Somme, when the British and French armies attacked the German positions on a front of twenty-five miles. Below, the British troops are seen "standing to"—waiting the order to advance. On the left one of the huge mines is seen exploding, hurling heavenwards its tons of earth and stones—the giant crater being later rushed by troops. In the first day's fighting the British troops captured over 3,500 prisoners. The Battle of the Somme was one of the great offensives of the War, and it continued until the end of November. The total British losses in this great battle were close on 500,000 men.

Photos : I.W.M.

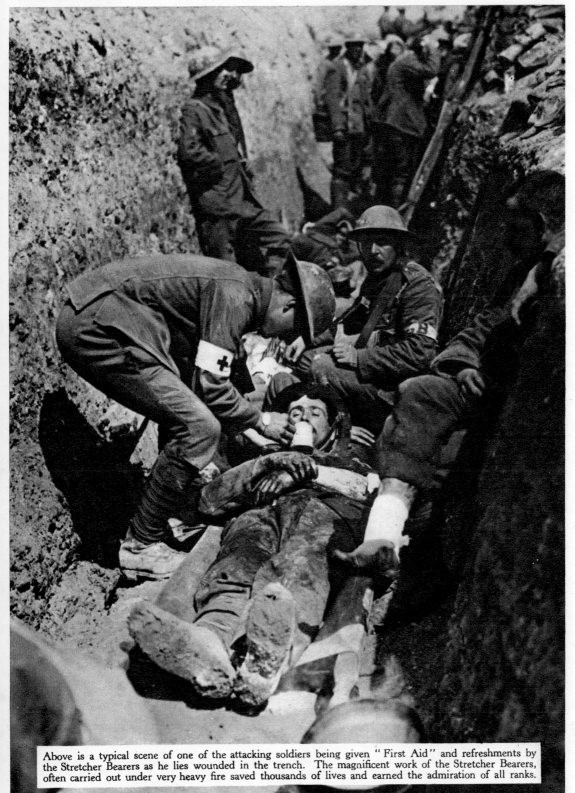

Above is a typical scene of one of the attacking soldiers being given "First Aid" and refreshments by the Stretcher Bearers as he lies wounded in the trench. The magnificent work of the Stretcher Bearers, often carried out under very heavy fire saved thousands of lives and earned the admiration of all ranks.

Photo : I.W.M.

ON the right are seen the curving flares of the star shells lighting the battlefield at night with their unearthly gleam; the opposing troops must be ever on the alert in case of a night attack or a raid.

Photos : I.W.M.

Above : The aftermath—the Roll Call with its tragic silences when familiar names are unanswered. After every attack a Roll Call was made at the earliest possible opportunity. So, the ever-mounting toll of war's carnage was revealed.

Photo : I.W.M.

Not cave-men, but men of the Border Regiment occupying the Front Line trenches in Thiepval Wood.   The holes they occupy were nick-named "funk-holes" as distinct from the larger "dug-outs."   Sand bags played a prominent part.

Keeping watch while his comrades are deep in the sleep of utter exhaustion. A scene in a front line trench—Ovillers.

Photo : I.W.M.

Gas masks gave the men a strange, almost terrifying appearance, as can be seen from these Australians in a trench at Garter Point, near Ypres. When the mask was not in use, it was replaced in the satchel which hung round the neck.

Photo : I.W.M.

A wiring party. There were few things more dangerous than to leave the shelter of the trench and crawl out across
No Man's Land in the darkness to erect barbed wire entanglements. The flare of a star shell made the men an easy target.

Photo : I.W.M.

On September 15, a carefully guarded secret was brought into the open, when for the first time British Tanks went into action in the Battle of the Somme. The Germans were taken completely by surprise, and the Kaiser and his Chief of Staff, Paul von Hindenburg (seen here consulting maps) were puzzled as to how they could combat this new form of warfare.

Waiting to go into action behind the tanks. In that first attack on September 15, 1916, a single tank with two companies of Infantry cleared a mile of trench and, apart from killed and wounded, 370 prisoners were taken with a loss of only five men.

Photos : I.W.M.

Here is one of the big guns that supported the troops during the long-drawn-out battle of the Somme. These great guns, capable of firing heavy shells many miles, were employed for bombarding important enemy positions well behind his front line. As may be seen, the gun is camouflaged to prevent it being "spotted" by enemy aircraft.

Photo : I.W.M.

Winter on the Western Front, 1916. An officer makes his rounds, wading through a trench of half-frozen mud.

FROST WAS
BETTER
THAN THIS!

On left: Horses knee-deep in mud, carrying ammunition along the Lesboeufs road to the forward guns.

Below: the scene of utter chaos and desolation outside a concrete "pill-box" that had been remorselessly shelled.

Photos: I.W.M.

Photo : I.W.M.

Prisoner of War! An expressive study of a young British soldier soon after capture and imprisonment in a German camp.

KEEPING THE HOME FIRES BURNING

THE constant call for more and more men meant that more and more vacancies were left to be filled by women. In this year the land-girls made their appearance. A few are seen at work in the top picture. The milk-woman on her daily rounds (right) was also a very familiar sight.

Photos : Topical

Lloyd George's unflagging efforts as Minister of Munitions resulted in a tremendous increase in the production of war material. In December of this year he became Prime Minister of the Coalition Government.

Photo : Cossira

Photos : I.W.M.

The guns whose supply of shells had been restricted were once more able to bring their full powers into play.   *Above :* a battery in action.   *Below :* behind the lines the vast ammunition dumps which did so much to increase confidence.

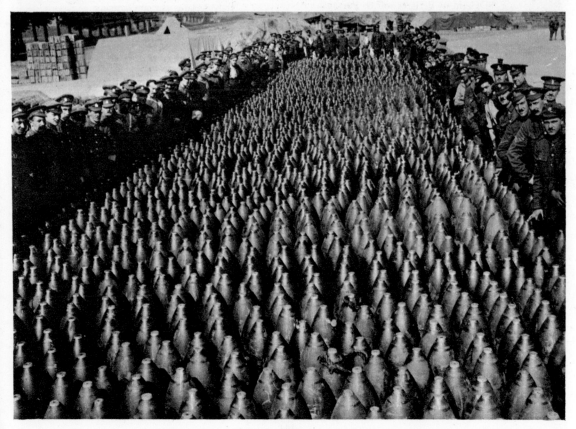

PRINCIPAL EVENTS OF 1916

JAN. 5. Conscription Bill introduced.

,, 8. Evacuation of Gallipoli completed.

,, 11. Mr. Herbert Samuel becomes Home Secretary.

,, 14. Lord Chelmsford made Viceroy of India.

,, 17. Escape of Tribitch Lincoln.

,, 23. Aeroplane raid on Kent.

,, 31. Zeppelin raid on East Coast. Six or seven Zeppelins over Midlands.

FEB. 3. Parliament buildings at Ottawa destroyed by fire.

,, 10. Compulsory military service for single men 19-30.

,, 18. Germans in Cameroons surrender.

,, 20. Aeroplane raid on East Coast.

,, 21. Battle of Verdun begun.

,, 28. Death of Henry James, novelist.

MAR. 2. Military Service Act comes into operation.

Death of Queen Elizabeth of Rumania.

,, 8. Germany declares war on Portugal.

,, 19. Seaplane raid, Deal, Dover, Margate and Ramsgate.

,, 27. In Paris, first War Conference of all the Allies.

APR. 1. Zeppelin brought down in Thames estuary.

,, 14. British aeroplanes raid Constantinople.

,, 15. Panama Canal reopened.

,, 19. Field Marshall von der Goltz dies.

,, 21. Sir Roger Casement arrested in Ireland.

,, 24. Outbreak of rebellion in Ireland.

,, 29. Fall of Kut after resistance of 143 days. General Townshend surrenders with 9,000 troops.

MAY 1. End of the Dublin rising.

,, 15. Sir Roger Casement tried for high treason.

,, 21. Summer Time Act comes into operation.

,, 25. Royal assent to Military Service Act No. 2

MAY 31. Arrival of Sir Ernest Shackleton at Falkland Islands from Southern Exploration Expedition.
Naval battle off Jutland.

JUNE 5. Lord Kitchener drowned in H.M.S. *Hampshire.*

General von Moltke dies.

,, 26. Jimmy Wilde wins fly-weight championship of Great Britain.

,, 29. Sir Roger Casement sentenced to death.

JULY 1. Anglo-French offensive on the Somme.

,, 6. Mr. Lloyd George appointed Secretary of State for War.

,, 9. Mr. E. S. Montagu appointed Minister of Munitions.

,, 26. Capt. Chas. Fryatt of G.E.R. Steamer *Brussels* sentenced to death by Germans.

,, 30. Zeppelin raids on South-east Counties.

AUG. 3. Execution of Sir Roger Casement.

,, 9. Zeppelin raid, Eastern England.

,, 27. Rumania declares war on Austria-Hungary.

,, 28. Germany declares war on Rumania.
Italy declares war on Germany.

,, 30. Field Marshal von Hindenburg appointed Chief of German Staff.

SEPT. 3. Schütte-Lanz Airship brought down at Cuffley.

,, 15. First use of tanks.

,, 23. Two Zeppelins brought down in Essex.

OCT. 1. Zeppelin raid; one brought down at Potters Bar.

,, 23. Sir Joseph Beecham dies, aged 68.

NOV. 21. Emperor Francis Joseph of Austria dies.

,, 29. Sir John Jellicoe appointed First Sea Lord and Admiral Sir D. Beatty in command of the Grand Fleet.

DEC. 4. Mr. J. H. Thomas appointed secretary of National Union of Railwaymen.

,, 5. Mr. Asquith resigns.

,, 7. Mr. Lloyd George becomes Prime Minister.

,, 11. M. Briand forms French War Ministry.

,, 29. Rasputin murdered.

Photo : I.W.M.

"TAKE COVER"

Photo : Topical

The food problem became acute for the housewife. The shops seemed empty and food was dear. Partial rationing came into force in June, though general rationing was not introduced until the following year—January 1, 1918.

Photo : I.W.M.

In contrast, these vast pyramids of army stores at Boulogne are an indication of the tremendous organisation needed to distribute food to troops extended over the Western Front. Whatever happened they were not allowed to go short.

Photo : I.W.M.

Mr. Clynes and Mr. Hoover were Food Controllers respectively for England and America. The latter is here seen with
Mr. Clynes, in conference for the adequate distribution of supplies during these critical months of intensive blockade.

Photo : Cossira

General Smuts, one of the outstanding figures of the War, is seen above. It is interesting to recall that the General who did such splendid work for us in Africa during the Great War, actually fought against us in the Boer War.

Photo : Cossira

War on land and sea—and now in the skies. Aircraft were taking a more and more important part in the fighting. The picture is of a seaplane in flames, having been shot down on to the sea after a fierce duel to the death in the clouds.

UNRESTRICTED SUBMARINE WARFARE

*T*HE policy of " unrestricted sub-marine warfare " as from February 1, was announced to neutral countries by Germany. The result was a considerable increase in the number of non-combatant vessels torpedoed by submarines.

Here are two photographs taken during this year. *Above :* a steamer sinking stern first under the waves. *Below :* a photo-graph taken at the actual moment a torpedo hits a helpless merchant vessel, showing the destructiveness of this weapon.

Photos : I.W.M.

Photo : Cossira

The crew of a doomed vessel are here seen leaving their ship. One of the most effective answers to the German blockade was a system of convoys for merchant vessels which gave enemy submarines much fewer opportunities for attack.

Photos : I.W.M.

Camouflage was used with success at sea. The vivid patterns made the real nature of the vessel difficult to distinguish at a distance. Here is a " dazzle " camouflaged troopship leaving the harbour at Boulogne. The men all wear lifebelts.

Photos : I.W.M.

In Palestine the fighting against the Turks went on amid conditions of heat and lack of water as terrible in their way as the mud of the Western Front. The top picture shows a party of Turks surrendering. *Below*, the Turkish prisoners, half-dead with thirst and exhaustion and under a pitiless sun, are being given some water by an English soldier.

Photo : Cossira

On December 9, Jerusalem surrendered to Lord Allenby, six months after he assumed command. After a series of swift victories that read like a page of Bible history—Gaza, Beersheba, Joppa, Hebron—the Holy City was captured.

In Russia the Tsar abdicated early in the year, and Russia was proclaimed a Socialist Republic with Kerensky as President and Commander-in-Chief. Supported by Germany, Lenin and Trotsky returned home to Russia from Switzerland.

Photo : Cossira

Trotsky was imprisoned, but Lenin incited the Communist party to action, and for the second time in one year, revolution
broke out.   This picture shows a crowd flying from a hail of bullets in Petrograd on the awful day when hostilities began.

THE NEW RULERS OF RUSSIA

*W*ITH the overthrow of Kerensky, Lenin and Trotsky ruled supreme and Bolshevism was established. Not many months were to elapse before Russia would withdraw from the War. The bottom picture shows the ill-fated Russian Royal Family, afterwards assassinated at Ekaterinburg on July 16, 1918. In the circle below is Lenin (Vladimir Ilyich Ulyanov), and on the left is his colleague Trotsky (Lev Bronstein).

Photos: Cossira

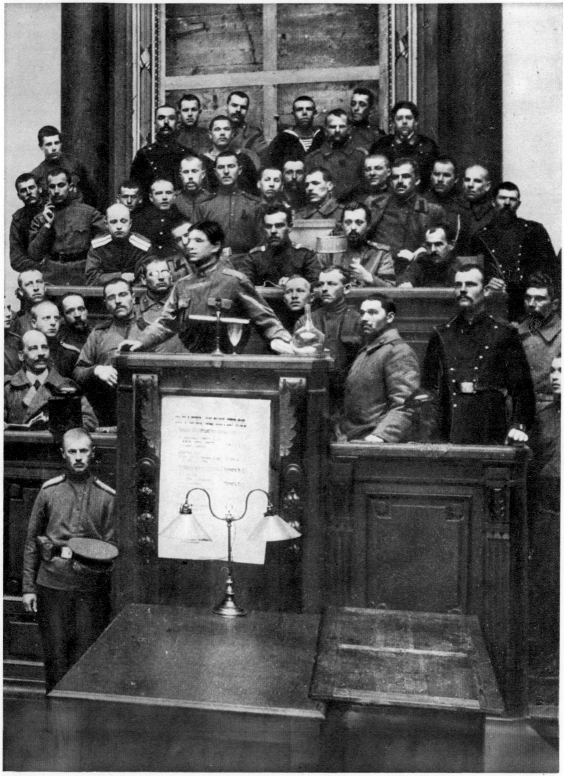

Photos : Cossira

Above is an interesting photograph of an assembly of one of the many "Soviets" which were formed throughout Russia.

Photo : I.W.M.

AMERICA
COMES
INTO THE WAR

*T*HE entrance on April 6 of America into the war, had a tremendous effect upon the *morale* of the Allies, especially France, who had barely recovered from Verdun and who witnessed with restored hope the arrival of a new and vigorous ally. Above is a photograph showing some of the early American troops. *Right* : General Pershing, Commander-in-Chief of the American forces, arrives in France.

Photo : Cossira

Photo : Topical

His Majesty the King attends a baseball match at Stamford Bridge, arranged in honour of the American allies.

This year Sir Arthur Lee (now Lord Lee of Fareham) presented "Chequers" to the nation as the official country residence of the Prime Minister. Above is a photograph of this beautiful residence which is in the county of Buckinghamshire.

During the summer, National Baby Week was inaugurated. The stringent conditions of wartime made it imperative that the children should have as much care lavished on them as possible if they were to grow up healthy. The health for babies campaign launched in that year did much important work both for mothers and their babies all over the land. *Above :* some of the prize-winning babies and children of the first National Baby Week with their mothers.

Photo: Topical

Periodically during the war, Investitures were held by the King.   In the presence of troops drawn up in ceremonial parade officers and men of all ranks received decorations for conspicuous service to their country !   H.M. the King is seen in the above photograph, decorating an officer with the Victoria Cross at an Investiture in Buckingham Palace Yard.

F.

This picture, which was taken on September 20, shows a typical scene on the Menin Road during the gigantic offensive made by the British armies in the Ypres Sector. The more seriously wounded lie on

Photo: I.W.M.

stretchers and are patiently awaiting removal to the "field" hospitals, while an endless stream of unaided "walking cases" make their tortuous journey as best they can along the shell shattered road on the way to the dressing station.

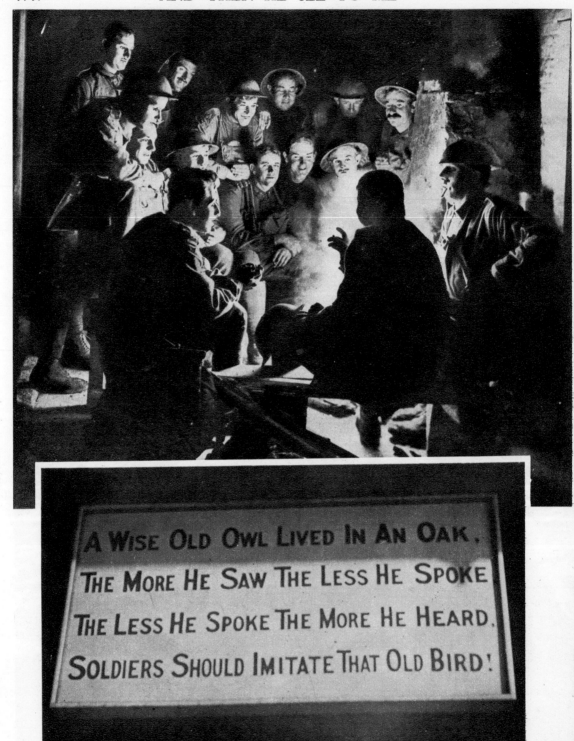

Photo: I.W.M.

Close round the fire they sit, laughing and talking, as if in the safety of their own homes, the horror of it all is momentarily forgotten. Even war had its relaxations. Below, however, is a good-humoured, but none the less serious warning, exhibited in stations and public places, that too much freedom of speech was dangerous—there were spies about.

The Entente Cordiale was evidenced in thousands of instances similar to the one illustrated by this photograph, where an elderly French couple are doing everything in their power to make the soldiers billeted upon them feel at home.

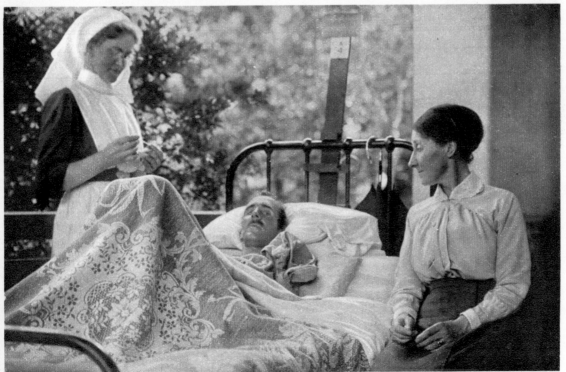

Photos: I.W.M.

A mother visits her son in hospital. Typical of countless visits bringing comfort to the wounded, this picture, taken at Le Touquet, reflects the atmosphere of the many hospitals and convalescent homes behind the front in the theatre of War.

PRINCIPAL EVENTS OF 1917

JAN. 1. Sir D. Haig created a Field-Marshal.
,, 9. Allies reply to President Wilson's Note.
,, 16. Death of Admiral George Dewey.

FEB. 3. U.S. breaks relations with Germany.
,, 5. Death of Paul Rubens.
,, 11. Death of Duke of Norfolk.
,, 24. Gen. Maude captures Kut-el-Amara.
,, 25. German retreat on the Ancre.
,, 28. British capture Gommecourt.

MAR. 8. Count Zeppelin dies aged 78.
,, 11. Gen. Maude captures Baghdad.
,, 12. Revolution in Russia.
,, 14. Duchess of Connaught dies.
,, 15. Abdication of Tsar Nicholas of Russia.
,, 17. British capture Bapaume.
    Resignation of M. Briand.
,, 18. Ramsgate and Broadstairs shelled from the sea.
,, 26. British attack Turks at Gaza.
,, 29. General Foch takes over Command of the whole of the Allied Armies.

APR. 5. U.S.A. declare war on Germany.
,, 7. Cuba declares war on Germany.
,, 9. British advance and capture Vimy Ridge.
,, 16. Food strikes in Germany.
,, 26. German naval raid on Ramsgate.

MAY 12. Men between 41 and 50 accepted for the army.
,, 13. Bus stoppage in London.
,, 15. General Petain appointed Commander of Northern and North Eastern French Armies on Western Front.
,, 18. Death of John Neville Maskelyne, illusionist.
,, 25. Aeroplanes raid Folkestone.
,, 27. Death of Leopold de Rothschild.
,, 29. Rt. Hon. Arthur Henderson, M.P., leaves on special mission to Russia.

JUNE 7. British capture Messines-Wytschaete Ridge.
,, 8. General Pershing arrives in London.
,, 11. Abdication of King Constantine of Greece.
,, 13. Aeroplanes raid London.
,, 21. Two new orders instituted open to both sexes; "Order of British Empire" and "Order of the Companions of Honour."
    Death of Sir Joseph Lyons.
,, 26. U.S. Troops in France.

JUNE 29. General Allenby appointed Commander in Palestine.
    Greece declares war on Germany.

JULY 2. Death of Sir Herbert Beerbohm Tree.
,, 7. Aeroplanes raid London and Margate; 97 killed, 193 injured.
,, 16. Revolution in Petrograd.
,, 21. Russian retreat.
,, 28. Tank Corps formed.

AUG. 10. Education Bill introduced by Mr. Fisher.
,, 11. Rt. Hon. Arthur Henderson, M.P., retires from War Cabinet.

SEPT. 3. Fall of Riga to Germans.
,, 14. German submarine shells Scarborough.
,, 15. Russia proclaimed a Republic.
,, 17. 9d. Loaf Order in force.

OCT. 1. Aeroplane raids on London.
,, 5. Sir Arthur Lee presents Chequers as official country residence for Prime Ministers.
,, 24. Death of Sir William Herschel, inventor of finger print identity system.
,, 31. General Allenby captures Beersheba.

NOV. 6. Canadians capture Passchendaele.
,, 7. Bolsheviks seize Government in Petrograd.
,, 16. M. Clemenceau becomes French Premier.
,, 17. General Allenby enters Jaffa.
,, 17. Naval engagement in Heligoland Bight.
,, 18. Rodin dies aged 77.
    General Maude dies.

DEC. 1. German East Africa cleared of German forces.
,, 8. Revolution in Portugal.
,, 10. General Allenby occupies Jerusalem.
,, 15. Russo-German armistice for month's truce signed at Brest-Litovsk.
,, 17. Death of Elizabeth Garrett Anderson, M.D., the first Englishwoman to be granted an English medical diploma.

1918

WOMEN TAKE OVER ON THE HOME FRONT

LONDON AND HOME COUNTIES.						Meat Card D 7.

Butcher's Names: (See Instructions overleaf.)
HALL AND SON (DURING FEBRUARY.)
GOSLIN AND CO.   MARCH.
J. RATCLIFF.   APRIL.
R. ALLEN AND CO.   MAY.

Butcher's Address

GIVE THIS PART TO YOUR BUTCHER.

9   9   9   9   10   10   10   10
11   11   11   11   12   12   12   12
13   13   13   13   14   14   14   14

MEAT CARD [L. and H.C.]

Office of Issue _____

A. Holder's Name :—
Her Majesty the Queen
Address :—
Buckingham Palace
S.W. 1

B. Holder's Signature :—
Mary R

C. Butcher's Name and Address :—

IF FOUND, DROP IN A PILLAR BOX.

20   20   15   15
20   20   15   15
19   19   16   16
19   19   16   16
18   18   17   17
18   18   17   17
8   8   8   8   7   7   7
6   6   6   6   5   5   5
4   4   4   4   3   3   3
2   2   2   2   1   1   1

LONDON AND HOME COUNTIES.						Meat Card D 7.

Butcher's Names: (See Instructions overleaf.)
HALL AND SON (DURING FEBRUARY.)
GOSLIN AND CO.   MARCH.
J. RATCLIFF.   APRIL.
R. ALLEN AND CO.   MAY.

Butcher's Address

GIVE THIS PART TO YOUR BUTCHER.

9   9   9   9   10   10   10   10
11   11   11   11   12   12   12   12
13   13   13   13   14   14   14   14

MEAT CARD [L. and H.C.]

Office of Issue _____

A. Holder's Name :—
His Majesty the King
Address :—
Buckingham Palace
S.W. 1

B. Holder's Signature :—
George R.I.

C. Butcher's Name and Address :—

IF FOUND, DROP IN A PILLAR BOX.

20   20   15   15
20   20   15   15
19   19   16   16
19   19   16   16
18   18   17   17
18   18   17   17
8   8   8   8   7   7   7
6   6   6   6   5   5   5
4   4   4   4   3   3   3
2   2   2   2   1   1   1

Photo: I.W.M

THE
FOOD
QUEUES

Carefully organised rationing came into force at the beginning of this year, and everyone from the highest to the lowest was supplied with ration cards available for meat, sugar, butter, etc. The cards above were issued to H.M. the King and Queen. Even with rationing, however, food was scarce. Housewives and their children formed queues and stood for hours to get their meagre supplies.

Photo : I.W.M.

An intensive campaign had started at home to obtain still more money and men. The way in which women were "doing their bit" is well symbolised by the woman-billposter sticking up the repeated exhortation to "Do It Now!"

WOMEN
STEP
INTO THE
BREECHES!

BY 1918 it was hard to imagine a single kind of job that had not been taken over by women. From the most delicate and complicated machinery to the equally important and skilful work of farming—there were women in every position. Above a pair of women painters are shown working on girders high above a busy street. On the right is a woman coalheaver. One minor concession to their sex was the introduction of 1 cwt. sacks instead of those usually weighing 2 cwt! Even this was not usual!

Photos: I.W.M.

DOING
MEN'S JOBS
AND
DOING THEM
VERY WELL !

On the left : A woman attends to the furnaces of a factory. *Below :* A better-known side of woman's war activities—ambulance drivers

Photo : I.W.M.

AT dawn on March 21, the Germans launched their long-awaited grand offensive against the British armies; this was Ludendorff's last desperate bid for victory before the American armies could become effective. The brunt of the attack was borne by the Fifth Army in the St. Quentin sector, though the enemy hurled many divisions at other sections of the line. The British armies sustained a serious blow, the casualties being over 300,000. The Germans advanced on a wide front, and for a time the British line was in peril. With the coming of reinforcements, and thanks to the heroism of the troops, irreparable disaster was averted. Before the final decision was reached, the titanic struggle between the opposing armies was to continue for many months with an intensity unparalleled in the annals of war. The picture shows a typical scene in the German front line trenches, with the Infantry preparing during the night for the attack at dawn.

Blinded and tortured with pain by poison gas.   A scene at a clearing station behind the line during the great offensive.

Photos : I.W.M.

" All that was left of them "—a German machine-gun crew wiped out.   They had fought and died defending their gun.

Photo: I.W.M.

As a result of the grave situation that had arisen owing to the German successes, it became imperative for the Allies to pool their resources, and after a conference at Doullens on March 29 attended by Mr. Lloyd George and the leading Allied statesmen, Foch was appointed Generalissimo on the Western Front—the unified command had come into being!

"WITH OUR BACKS TO THE WALL
WE MUST FIGHT ON TO THE END"

Above is Field-Marshal Sir Douglas Haig, Commander-in-Chief of the British forces on the Western Front since 1915. No man better realised the gravity of the position in the early months of 1918. His stirring message to the troops which is reproduced on the right, inspired the whole army in the hour of crisis. Although the Germans launched further terrific attacks, the line was never again seriously in danger.

To / All ranks of the British Forces in France

Three weeks ago today the Enemy began his terrific attacks against us on a 50 mile front. His objects are to separate us from the French, to take the Channel ports and destroy the British army.

Despite of throwing already 106 Divisions into the battle and ~~suffering~~ enduring the most reckless sacrifice of human life, he has as yet made little progress towards his goals.

We owe this to the determined fighting & self sacrifice of our troops. Words fail me to express the admiration which I feel for the splendid resistance offered by all ranks of our army under the most trying circumstances.

Many amongst us now are ~~~~ tired. To these I would say that Victory will belong to the side which holds out the longest. The French army is moving rapidly & in great force to our support - - - - -

. There is no other course open to us but to fight it out! Every position must be held to the last man: there must be no retirement -. With our backs to the wall and believing in the justice of our cause Each one of us must fight on to the End. The safety of our Homes and the Freedom of mankind alike depend upon the conduct of each one of us at this critical moment. ~~But be of Good cheer, the British Empire~~ ~~remains in the End~~ ..

D. Haig. F. M.

Thursday,
11 April 1918

Photo : Topical

Photo : I.W.M.

More money was needed to carry on. The top photo shows Trafalgar Square, transformed into a model battlefield to stir the imagination of those at home in order to increase contributions to the War Loan. Meanwhile, on the Western Front new drafts and reinforcements were concentrating at points from which fresh attacks were expected.

Photo : G.P.A.

During their great offensive, the Germans, with the intention of breaking the morale of civilians, introduced the amazing long-range gun which was nicknamed " Big Bertha," from Frau Bertha von Bohlen und Halbach, principal proprietor of Krupp's factory. This gun, which is seen above, shelled Paris from the Forest of Coucy, a distance of 76 miles.

THE
RAID
ON
ZEEBRUGGE

ON April 23, 1918, a British force under Commander A. F. B. Carpenter in H.M.S. *Vindictive* sailed for Zeebrugge, directed by Admiral Sir Roger Keyes, who had conceived the daring plan of bottling up the German submarines by sinking British ships filled with concrete, at the entrance to the harbour. After incredible hardships, this was effected.

On the left is Sir Roger Keyes, and below : One of the derelict ships with the Mole, which was the centre of the scene of operations, in the background.

Photo : I.W.M.

Photo : Topical

Above : An aerial view of the entrance to Zeebrugge Harbour, clearly showing the sunken ships blocking the entrance.

Below : The battle-scarred *Vindictive* on her triumphant return to Dover under her own steam, after the famous raid.

Photos : I.W.M.

Photo : I.W.M.

Aircraft continued to play a more and more important part in the War. By means of daring raids over the enemy lines, much valuable information was obtained and much damage done. The picture shows a bombing squadron drawn up at St. Omer.

In this year a remarkable experiment was successfully carried out, when an aeroplane was launched off a carrier towed behind a cruiser enabling fighting planes to start their attacks nearer their objectives without depletion of petrol supplies.

Photos : I.W.M

A wrecked allied aeroplane near Cherisy. A spectacle that normally would attract huge crowds, but so common had such sights as wrecked aeroplanes become that the damaged machine excited little interest in the passing troops.

Their Majesties celebrated their Silver wedding on July 6th. This group was taken at Buckingham Palace to commemorate the occasion.

Prince Albert   Prince George
H.M. The Queen

Prince Henry H.M. The King Princess Mary

Photo: Cen Press

A bombardment during the battle of the Marne, 1918, when the Germans were relinquishing the ground which the gained at so great a price in their final rush towards Paris. Overhead a German biplane is patrolling the forward

British tank can be seen advancing in the background. The flag on the left is a signal for patrolling 'planes. This picture gives some idea of the devastating horror of warfare, when modern Armies are grappling for mastery.

Photo : I.W.M.

Photo: I.W.M.

At long last! In the summer the tide began to turn and the German retreat began. Here, the picture shows the Canadian troops advancing steadily over very open ground in pursuit of the now demoralised enemy.

The 4th Seaforth Highlanders investigating a dug-out in the recently captured German front lines after the Battle of the Scarpe in August. They are seen at the dugout's exit shouting a warning to any possible fugitive to surrender.

Photos : I.W.M.

Through long lanes of cheering women and children—the only civilians left to welcome them. The victorious entry of the Liverpool Irish into the recaptured town of Lille on October 18. A memorable milestone on the road to final victory.

Photo : S. & G

A scene in Whitehall at 11 o'clock on November 11th, 1918, when it was known that at long last hostilities had ceased.

Photo : Cossina

German officers carrying a white flag approach a British Brigade Headquarters. Their task was to act as guides to the
British officers who were taking over after the "cease fire" had been given, and to lead them safely over mine-infested areas.

London never witnessed a more spontaneous demonstration of joy than on November 11th, 1918. At last, at the eleventh hour of the eleventh day of the month, had come the end of the War which had in some way or another affected every household, and people everywhere left their offices and homes to celebrate in the streets the coming of Peace.

This photograph was taken at the Royal Exchange, and is typical of scenes that were taking place all over the country. And among the many thousands of men and women who thronged the streets cheering—or weeping—with relief that the War was at last over, there were many of those who had cheered, over four years before, because war had been declared.

A scene which sums up the tragedy of the devastated area.
A child crying over the wrecked treasures of her home.

Photo : I.W.M.

UNDER the terms of the Armistice the greater part of the German Fleet was surrendered, and it was decided to intern it in Scapa Flow. This photograph taken from the air, shows H.M.S. *Queen Elizabeth* leading in the long line of surrendered ships.

Photo : I.W.M.

The sequel to the surrender of the German Fleet came on June 21, 1919, when the interned ships were scuttled. The German skeleton crew, at a pre-arranged signal, opened the sea-cocks, making good their escape as the ships sank.

Photos : I.W.M.

The top picture shows one of the ships slowly settling down, and, below, is a photograph of another heeling over as she sinks. Notice one of the German crew balancing himself as the ship lists, and the tug alongside waiting to rescue him.

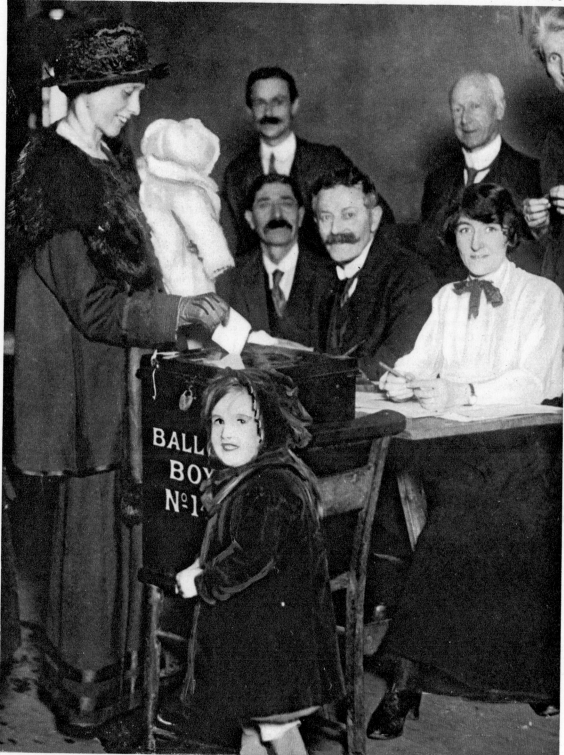

Photo : Topical

In the General Election on December 14, 1918, women for the first time exercised the vote for which they had fought for years. In this election, which returned the Coalition Government, women over thirty were on the register.

PRINCIPAL EVENTS OF 1918

FEB. 2. Death of John Lawrence Sullivan, famous prize fighter.

,, 6. Representation of the People Bill receives Royal Assent.

,, 18. Hostilities between Germany and Russia re-commence.
Lord Northcliffe appointed Director of Propaganda in enemy countries.

,, 21. British troops occupy Jericho.

,, 25. Rationing of meat, butter and margarine comes into force in London and Home Counties.

MAR. 6. Death of John Redmond, leader of the Irish party in the Commons.

,, 13. Odessa occupied by Germans : Petrograd evacuated.

,, 16. Death of Sir George Alexander, actor manager.

,, 18. Germans repulsed on Belgian front.

,, 21. Great German attack from Scarpe to Oise.

,, 22. General Allenby crosses the Jordan.

,, 23. Paris shelled by Big Bertha.

,, 26. Death of Claude Debussy, the French composer.

APR. 2. The Prince of Wales is made first Chancellor of new South African University of Capetown.

,, 16. General Foch appointed Generalissimo of the Allied Armies in France.

,, 23. Successful Naval Raid on Zebrugge under Vice-Admiral Roger Keyes.

MAY 7. Rumania signs "Peace of Bucharest."

,, 14. Death of James Gordon Bennett, owner of New York Herald.

JUNE 3. Postage rate raised to 1½d. for letter, 1d. for postcards.

,, 23. Great Austrian defeat.

JULY 3. Viscount Rhondda dies aged 62.
Death of Sultan of Turkey.

JULY 6. Their Majesties' silver wedding.

,, 10. Mr. J. R. Clynes appointed Food Controller.

,, 16. Ex-Czar of Russia Nicholas Romanoff shot.

,, 19. Mr. Hoover, U.S. Food Controll arrived in London.

AUG. 3. Australia House opened by the King.

6. General Foch created a Marshal of France.

,, 15. British troops cross the Ancre.

,, 30. British cross the Somme.

SEPT. 20. General Allenby occupies Nazareth.

,, 26. Franco-American victory on the Meuse.

,, 27. British break Hindenburg line at Cambrai.

OCT. 13. German retreat on a 100-mile front.

,, 30. Conference at Versailles of Allied Chiefs.

,, 31. Government Bill making women eligible for Parliament introduced in House of Commons.

NOV. 9. Abdication of the Kaiser announced.

,, 10. Revolution in Berlin.

,, 11. Armistice with Germany signed. Hostilities ceased at 11 a.m.

,, 14. Professor Masaryk elected First President of Czecho-Slovak Republic.

,, 21. German Fleet surrenders to Britain.

,, 29. King Nicholas of Montenegro deposed and country united with Serbia under King Peter.

DEC. 13. President Wilson landed in France for the Peace Conference.

,, 14. General Election. Women vote for first time.
Assassination of President of Portuguese Republic at Lisbon.

,, 28. Victory of Coalition Government in General Election.

(From the painting by Sir William Orpen, R.A.)

THE TREATY OF VERSAILLES

Early in 1919, Eamon De Valera, one of the foremost figures in Irish politics, escaped with two other prominent leaders, from Lincoln Gaol, where he had been imprisoned in May, 1918, on a charge of attempting to organise a Sinn Fein

Photo : Central Press

rising in Ireland. He and his followers had now become extremely active, adding greatly to the after war problems of the government. This unique photograph shows De Valera taking the salute of the Sinn Feiners as they march past.

Photo : S. & G.

The Atlantic was crossed by aeroplane for the first time on June 14, 1919, when Captain John Alcock and Lieutenant Arthur Whitten Brown flew from St. John's, Newfoundland, to Clifden, Ireland, in 16 hours 12 minutes. They were both knighted for their achievement. Here they are being given a tumultuous welcome after their historic flight.

Between July 2 and July 6, R.34 flew from East Fortune (near Edinburgh) to Long Island, America, and on July 9 started on the return journey to Pulham, Norfolk, arriving July 13—the first crossings made by a dirigible.

Photos : S. & G. (England)

Later in the year, Captain Ross Smith (third from the left), his brother (second from the left), and two companions completed the first aeroplane flight from England to Australia, thus winning the £10,000 prize awarded by the Australian Government. Their 'plane left England on November 12 and arrived at Port Darwin, Australia, on December 10.

A SCENE AT THE HISTORIC CONFERENCE AT VERSAILLES, WHERE THE PEACE TRE

Photo: Topical

DRAWN UP AND WHERE THE LEAGUE OF NATIONS WAS BROUGHT INTO BEING.

Photo : Topical

Peace was officially proclaimed from St. James's Palace after the signing on June 28 by Germany and the Allies of the Treaty of Versailles. The Treaty was brought into force by exchange of ratifications on January 10, 1920.

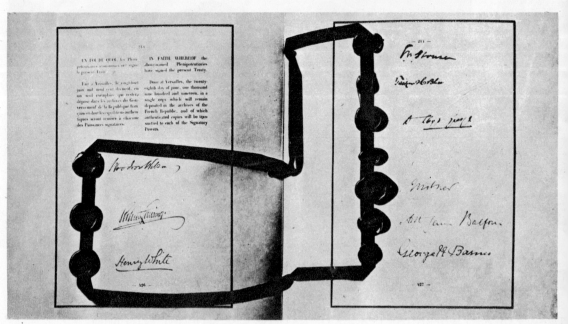

Photo : Cossira

Here is part of the famous document itself with the signatures of the representatives of the combatant countries.

THE
PEACE
MARCH

THE Peace Procession of July 19 was one of the most impressive spectacles ever witnessed. Contingents of all the allied forces took part, and all the great leaders either rode or marched step by step with the men. The top picture on the right shows Sir Douglas Haig —Commander-in-Chief of the British armies in France—in the procession. He was created Earl Haig later in the year. Below, is the march past of the famous "Old Contemptibles."

SALUTE TO THE FALLEN

ADMIRAL BEATTY during the Peace March leads the naval contingent past the temporary Cenotaph which had been erected in Whitehall. All ranks as they marched past the Cenotaph, saluted "The Glorious Dead."

209

All over the country the people celebrated the Peace.

Photo : Central Press

In every town could be witnessed scenes similar to this.

Photo : S. & G.

For nine days, from September 27 to October 6, the Great Railway Strike paralysed the country's transport. The regular delivery of newspapers was interrupted, and the resultant lack of news gave rise to many fantastic rumours.

Photo : " Flight "

On August 25, further advance in transport was made by the inauguration of the first regular London-to-Paris air service.

Photo : " Daily Herald "

Women Police were now a familiar feature of London life. A watchful eye being kept on youthful paddlers in the Serpentine.

Photo : S. & G.

A photograph taken at the scene of the first observance of the Two Minutes' Silence ceremony on Armistice Day, 1919, at the temporary Cenotaph in Whitehall. The permanent memorial, as known to-day, was not completed and unveiled until 1920.

Photo : Topical

A picture showing the scene in Piccadilly during the first Great Silence on November 11, 1919.   The traffic everywhere came to a standstill, engines of 'buses and cars were switched off, and vast crowds stood reverently in the streets.

Photo : I.W.M.

The Watch on the Rhine. A striking picture which shows two British soldiers, part of the Army of Occupation, looking down on the river at Cologne. For them and their comrades in the garrison, war duties were not yet over.

Photo : Topical

With the commencement of demobilisation, the women began to relinquish the positions they had held during the War years. Here is seen a woman conductor saying good-bye to her colleague. A man will take her place to-morrow.

Photo : Topical

On December 1, Viscountess Astor after a strenuous Election Campaign, took her seat in the Commons. The first woman M.P.

PRINCIPAL EVENTS OF 1919

JAN. 1. £1,000,000 damage by fire at Bethnal Green Food Warehouse.

,, 6. Death of Mr. Theodore Roosevelt.

,, 10. Mr. Churchill appointed Secretary of State for War.

,, 12. Death of Sir Charles Wyndham, actor-manager.

,, 18. First meeting of Peace Conference in Paris.

,, 19. Monarchist rising in Portugal. Monarchy proclaimed at Oporto.

FEB. 11. Herr Ebert assumed office as First President of German Republic.

MAR. 20. Wireless telephone communication established between Ireland and Canada.

,, 31. Jimmy Wilde defeated Joe Linch (U.S.A.).
First issue of *The Daily Herald*.

APR. 25. Formation of League of Nations approved by delegates to the Peace Congress at Versailles.

MAY 1. Civil flying to be permitted.

JUNE 4. Derby won by Lord Glanely's Grand Parade.

,, 14. Capt. John Alcock and Lieut. Whitten Brown fly North Atlantic.

,, 21. German fleet sunk at Scapa Flow.

,, 25. Rt. Hon. Christopher Addison appointed first Minister of Health.

,, 28. Germany signs Peace Treaty.

JULY 1. Prohibition adopted in U.S.A.

,, 4. Jack Dempsey beats Jess Willard for Heavy Weight Boxing Championship of the World.

,, 6. British airship R.34 flies to Long Island.

,, 13. R.34 lands at Pulham after double flight across the Atlantic.

JULY 17. Jimmy Wilde beats Pal Moore (U.S.A.).

AUG. 5. Prince of Wales leave to Tour Canada and U.S.A.

,, 9. Death of R. Leoncavallo, operatic composer.

,, 11. Death of Mr. Andrew Carnegie.

,, 25. London—Paris daily air service inaugurated.

,, 27. Death of General Louis Botha.

SEPT. 2. Joe Beckett beats McGoorty (U.S.A.).

,, 6. Death of Lord Beresford.

,, 10. Peace signed with Austria at St. Germain.

,, 12. Italians under Gabriele D'Annunzio occupy Fiume.

,, 27. Evacuation of Archangel by British troops.

OCT. 7. Disbandment of Women's Royal Air Force.

,, 10. King signs Peace Treaty.

,, 17. Death of H. B. Irving, actor-manager.

,, 20. Death of Ella Wheeler Wilcox.

NOV. 10. Air Mail starts between London and Paris.

,, 11. First Armistice Anniversary and Two Minutes Silence.

DEC. 1. Prince of Wales arrives home from Canada and U.S.A.
Lady Astor, the first woman to do so, takes her seat in the House of Commons.

,, 2. Death of Field Marshal Sir Evelyn Wood, V.C.

,, 4. Georges Carpentier knocks out Joe Beckett.

,, 10. Capt. Ross Smith completes London-Australia flight in just under 28 days.

,, 18. Sir John Alcock killed in aeroplane crash.

,, 19. Attempt on life of Lord French in Dublin.

,, 27 All British air route from Cairo to the Cape available for traffic.

THE HOUSING SHORTAGE

GROWING POPULARITY OF MOTORING

*T*HOUGH motor designing had made such strides, service facilities for motorists were still primitive. Here is the very first filling-station opened in this country at Aldermaston, Berks. Nothing, however, could hinder the triumphal progress of motoring and motor transport. The charabanc, the motor bus, and the cheap car had come to stay and became serious rivals to the railways. Below is a scene at the Derby of this year. Notice the amount of vehicular traffic. The number who travel to Epsom by car is increasing every year.

Photo by courtesy A.A.

Photo : Topical

His Royal Highness Prince Albert
was this year created Duke of York

On June 10, Their Majesties held their first court since 1914. London's " season " had regained its pre-war splende

Photo : Topical

is a photograph of the Throne Room at Buckingham Palace, where the debutantes are presented to the King and Queen. .

EARLY DAYS OF RADIO

*B*ROADCASTING was making great progress. The top picture shows the cumbersome transmitter which was still in use at Caernarvon in 1919. The lower picture, taken at Chelmsford in 1920, though still comparatively primitive is much more advanced. Here the announcer is giving the "news bulletin" from an evening newspaper. He is sitting beside the transmitter. Notice, too, the type of microphone that was used then in announcing.

Photos: Marconi

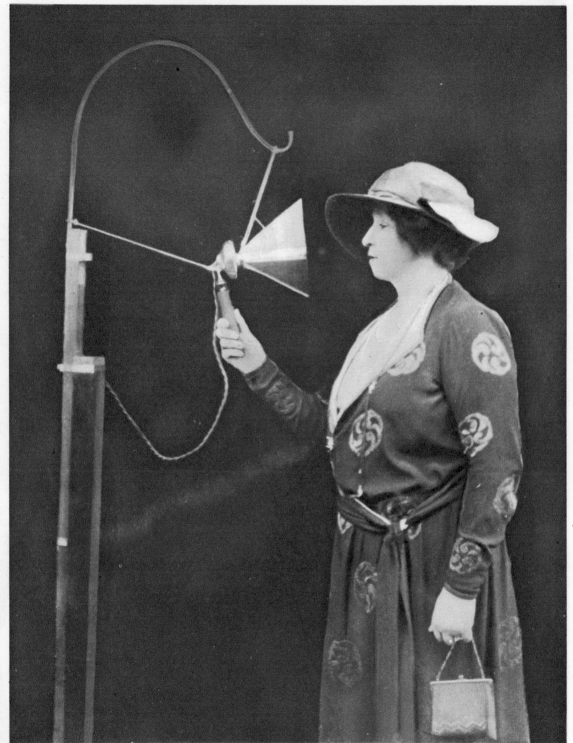

Photo : Marconi

Dame Nellie Melba made her first broadcast in 1920 from Chelmsford.   She was the first great operatic celebrity to risk the possible distortion of her voice over the wireless.   The experiment was successful.   Many people, including those who had never heard her voice before, "listened in" and were thrilled with the singing of the "Australian Nightingale."

"LEST WE FORGET"

AN impressive ceremony took place on Armistice Day, November 11, when the King unveiled the permanent Cenotaph—the Empty Tomb—in Whitehall. His Majesty is seen on the right pressing the button that released the Union Jacks draping the memorial. The unveiling of the Cenotaph was followed by the ceremony of the burial in State of the Unknown Warrior in Westminster Abbey.

Photo : Central Press

BENEATH THIS STONE RESTS THE BODY
OF A BRITISH WARRIOR
UNKNOWN BY NAME OR RANK
BROUGHT FROM FRANCE TO LIE AMONG
THE MOST ILLUSTRIOUS OF THE LAND
AND BURIED HERE ON ARMISTICE DAY
11 NOV: 1920 IN THE PRESENCE OF
HIS MAJESTY KING GEORGE V
HIS MINISTERS OF STATE
THE CHIEFS OF HIS FORCES
AND A VAST CONCOURSE OF THE NATION

THUS ARE COMMEMORATED THE MANY
MULTITUDES WHO DURING THE GREAT
WAR OF 1914-1918 GAVE THE MOST THAT
MAN CAN GIVE LIFE ITSELF
FOR GOD
FOR KING AND COUNTRY
FOR LOVED ONES HOME AND EMPIRE
FOR THE SACRED CAUSE OF JUSTICE AND
THE FREEDOM OF THE WORLD

THEY BURIED HIM AMONG THE KINGS BECAUSE HE
HAD DONE GOOD TOWARD GOD AND TOWARD
HIS HOUSE

IN CHRIST SHALL ALL BE MADE ALIVE

"THEY BURIED HIM AMONGST THE KINGS"

THE body of the Unknown Warrior was brought from the Western Front and on Armistice Day of this year was buried in Westminster Abbey. Above is the moving inscription on the grave, and below is the tomb in the Abbey, guarded by four representatives of the fighting forces.

Westminster Abbey is the resting place of many of Great Britain's Kings and Queens, and of many of her most illustrious sons. But no grave is revered more highly by the people of the nation than that of the unknown hero who represents the million men who laid down their lives for their country in the Great War.

PRINCIPAL EVENTS OF 1920

JAN. 12. French liner *L'Afrique* founders with 465 passengers on board.

,, 16. First meeting of the Council of the League of Nations held in Paris.

,, 17. Prohibition comes into force in America.

,, 21. W. C. F. Redmond, Deputy Assistant Commissioner of Police, assassinated in Dublin street.

,, 23. Netherlands Government decline to give up the Ex-Kaiser.

FEB. 11. First meeting in England of the League of Nations,

,, 19. Admiral Robert Edwin Peary, discoverer of North Pole, dies aged 63.

,, 26. U.S.S.R. sends new Peace offers to Allies.

MAR. 1. Death of Charles Garvice, popular novelist.

,, 16. Prince of Wales leaves for tour of Australia and New Zealand.

,, 17. Queen Alexandra unveils statue of Nurse Cavell in London.

,, 20. Lord Mayor of Cork, a Sinn Fein leader, shot dead in his house.

,, 24. Death of Mrs. Humphry Ward, novelist.

,, 27. Cambridge wins the Boat Race.

MAY 10. Joe Beckett knocks out Bombardier Wells.

,, 11. Convocation at Oxford passes statute making women eligible for degrees.

17. Express Air Mail service opened between London and Amsterdam.

,, 18. Devonshire House sold for one million guineas.

.. 28. Their Majesties lay the foundation stone of the new building, London School of Economics.

,, 29. Flood disaster in Lincolnshire.

JUNE 1. Postage rates for letters raised from 1½d. to 2d.
First Archbishop of Wales enthroned at St. Asaph.

,, 2. Derby won by Spion Kop—owned by Capt. Loder.

,, 10. First Court since 1914 held at Buckingham Palace.

,, 15. Dame Nellie Melba's first broadcast from Chelmsford.

,, 24. 700th Anniversary of Salisbury Cathedral.

JULY 1. German Airship L71 arrives at Pulham, having been handed over to Great Britain.

,, 10. Death of Admiral Lord Fisher.

,, 11. Death of Ex-Empress Eugenie of the French.

,, 16. Joe Beckett beat Tom Burns for heavyweight championship of the Empire.

,, 27. *Resolute* wins final race against *Shamrock* for the American Cup. America wins.

AUG. 2. Lieuts. Parer and MacIntosh arrive at Port Darwin, Australia.

,, 5. Two German dreadnoughts and twelve destroyers, surrendered at Kiel, brought to Rosyth.

,, 10. Peace signed with Turkey at Sèvres.

,, 20. H.M.S. *Vindictive* successfully refloated and towed into her berth at Ostend.

SEPT. 15. New Air Mail inaugurated between Copenhagen to Hamburg, Amsterdam and London.

OCT. 14. First degrees conferred on women at Oxford.

NOV. 11. Unknown Warrior buried in Westminster Abbey. (Over 1,000,000 people pass Cenotaph and Tomb.)

,, 15. Prince Arthur of Connaught, as new Governor-General of South Africa, lands at Cape Town.
League of Nation's first meeting at Geneva.

,, 30. King and Queen of Denmark arrive in London.

DEC. 4. Prohibition defeated in Scotland.

,, 8. Cambridge University refuse admission of women students to full membership.

,, 10. Frank Moran (U.S.A.) knocks out Joe Beckett.

,, 15. Austria admitted to the League of Nations.

,, 18. Restoration of King Constantine to Greek throne.

,, 20. Farrow's Bank suspends payment.

,, 21. Thomas Farrow, chairman of Farrow's Bank, arrested.

,, 29. *Chu Chin Chow* at His Majesty's Theatre beats all stage records with 2,000th performance.

1921

FROM WAR TO PEACE—BREAKING UP THE BATTLESHIPS

Photo : S. & G.

An eclipse of the sun this year aroused more than usual interest, since the weather permitted the phenomenon to be observed clearly. Here are some schoolboys being instructed by their master, while they gaze at the sun through smoked glass. The eclipse ended at ten in the morning, so that for many children it provided a happy break from lessons !

In March, 1921, Mr. Bonar Law, who was Mr. Lloyd George's right-hand man in the Coalition Government, had to retire from active politics for reasons of health. Mr. Austen Chamberlain (above) became in his place leader of the House of Commons and of the Conservative Party, in which position he remained till the Coalition Government fell in 1922.

A special session of Parliament to deal with the Irish situation was this year opened by the King. Mr. Whitley, seen above in his official robes, proved an exceptionally popular Speaker. He was elected to this important office on April 27.

Photo : A. W. Kerr

A remarkable picture taken inside the House of Lords, showing Their Majesties' thrones. It is from here that the King makes his speech to the Lords and Commons at the state opening of Parliament.

Photo : S. & G.

Two important ceremonies were performed by His Majesty the King during the summer. On June 6, he opened the new Southwark Bridge (seen in the lower picture) and a month later, on July 8, the new King George V Dock, London, was opened to shipping. The King is seen above shaking hands with one of the workmen during this ceremony.

Photo : Topical

In June, His Majesty travelled to Belfast, where, on the 22nd, the Parliament of Northern Ireland was opened with due ceremony. The Home Rule Act of 1920 had divided Ireland into two sections (now known as Northern Ireland and the Irish Free State) which were henceforth to have individual governments. The picture shows the Parliament Buildings at Belfast and the streets decorated for the occasion.

The KING
OPENS
the
NORTHERN
IRELAND
PARLIAMENT

Photos: S. & G.

The top picture shows Sir James Craig, the first Premier of Northern Ireland, awaiting the King, who performed the ceremony of opening the Northern Ireland Parliament; below, the King and Queen acknowledging the greetings of the crowd.

238

...months from the date hereof.

This instrument shall be submitted forthwith by His Majesty's Government for the approval of Parliament and by the Irish signatories to a meeting summoned for the purpose of the members elected to sit in the House of Commons of Southern Ireland, and if approved shall be ratified by the necessary legislation.

Decr 6th 1921.

On behalf of the British Delegation

D. Lloyd George
Austen Chamberlain.
Birkenhead.

Winston S. Churchill
L. Worthington-Evans
Hamar Greenwood
Gordon Hewart.

On behalf of the Irish Delegation

Art Ó Gríobhtha (Arthur Griffith)
Mícheál Ó Coileáin
Riobárd Barton
E. S. Ó Dúgáin
Seoirse Gabhán Uí Dhubhthaigh.

Photo : Topical

When this historic document, establishing the Irish Free State, was signed on December 6, it was hoped that Ireland would at last see peace. There were, however, many troublesome times ahead and many difficult problems to be solved.

Photo: *Topical*

DISASTER TO WORLD'S LARGEST AIRSHIP

A grave airship disaster occurred on August 24, when the R.38, then the largest airship in the world, broke up in the air and fell into the Humber in flames. Forty-four of her complement of forty-nine were killed. This photograph shows wreckage being lifted by cranes from the river. The airship had been sold to America and several victims were Americans.

KING IN HAPPY MOOD AT TEST MATCH

From the film, " Soul of a Nation "

The Test Matches with Australia were played in England for the first time since the War, and witnessed by enthusiastic crowds who had not seen the famous contest for the " Ashes " for many years. The King is here seen chatting happily to the two teams. In this series of tests Australia won three matches out of the five—the other two matches being drawn.

Photo : Cen. Press

The Prince of Wales set out on his Indian tour on October 26. He is seen here during his visit in the uniform of a colonel of the 34/35th Jacobs' Horse. This tour was very extensive and he also visited other countries, including Japan.

THE PRINCE OF WALES VISITS INDIA

THE State trumpeters (above) blow a welcoming fanfare to the Prince on his arrival at Mysore.

Right: natives from the little villages watch with enthusiastic interest as the royal train makes its journey through the country.

243

Photos: Central Press

PRINCIPAL EVENTS OF 1921

JAN. 7. First woman foreman of a jury at Dudley.

,, 8. Lord Reading appointed Viceroy of India.

FEB. 5. Death of Katharine Parnell (Mrs. O'Shea of the Parnell scandal).

,, 9. Duke of Connaught at Delhi inaugurates the two new Indian legislative Chambers—Council of State and Legislative Assembly.

,, 10. Peace Treaty signed between Poland and U.S.S.R.

,, 12. Winston Churchill appointed Secretary of State for Colonies.

,, 15. Duke of Connaught lays foundation stone of Indian Houses of Parliament at Delhi.

MAR. 4. Warren G. Harding installed President of the U.S.A.

,, 7. Mayor and Ex-Mayor of Limerick shot dead.

,, 11. Prince Arthur of Connaught opens New Union Parliament.

,, 17. Bonar Law resigns Leadership of Unionist Party.

,, 19. Daily Air Service to and from Paris resumed.

,, 30. Cambridge wins the Boat Race.

,, 31. Coal Stoppage (midnight). "State of Emergency" proclaimed April 1.

APR. 11. Death of Ex-Empress of Germany.

,, 14. Air Service commences between London and Amsterdam.

,, 27. Rt. Hon. J. H. Whitley elected Speaker of House of Commons.

MAY 25. Miss Olive Clapham becomes the first woman barrister.

Dublin Customs House, which cost £400,000 to build, destroyed by fire by Sinn Feiners. Over 100 arrests made.

JUNE 1. Mr. J. B. Joel's Humorist won the Derby.

,, 3. Lord Byng of Vimy appointed Governor General of Canada.

,, 6. King opens new Southwark Bridge.

,, 19. Census taken of Great Britain.

,, 22. The King opens Northern Ireland Parliament.

,, 29. Death of Lady Randolph Churchill.

JULY 2. Jack Dempsey knocked out Georges Carpentier at Jersey City, U.S.A., for championship of the world.

,, 4. King and Queen of Belgium arrive on state visit.
Coal stoppage settled.

,, 8. His Majesty opened new George V Dock.

,, 22. *Chu Chin Chow* comes to an end after 2,238 performances.

,, 27. Plans adopted by Imperial Conference for Imperial Wireless Chain.

AUG. 2. Death of Enrico Caruso.

,, 15. Government control of the railways comes to an end.

,, 16. King Peter of Yugoslavia died at Belgrade.

,, 24. R.38 disaster at Hull.

,, 25. Peace Treaty signed between the U.S.A. and Germany.

,, 31. Death of Field-Marshal Karl von Bulow.

SEPT. 5. Second assembly of the League of Nations opened at Geneva.

,, 11. Admiral of the Fleet, Lord Milford Haven, formerly Prince Louis of Battenberg, dies suddenly.

,, 17. Antarctic expedition—*Quest* sails—leader Sir Ernest Shackleton.

,, 27. Death of Engelbert Humperdinck, German composer.

,, 28. Lieut. John Macready breaks world's height record in a biplane, reaching 40,800 ft.

OCT. 14. Kid Lewis beat Johnny Basham for Middleweight Championship of Great Britain and Europe.

,, 17. Death of Ex-King Ludwig of Bavaria.

,, 23. Death of John Boyd Dunlop—inventor of pneumatic tyres.

,, 26. Prince of Wales sails for India.

NOV. 29. Death of Ivan Caryll, composer.

DEC. 6. Ireland given Dominion status.

,, 9. Death of Sir Arthur Pearson, Bart., Founder of St. Dunstan's.

,, 16. Saint-Saens, French composer, died.

,, 28. Death of Sir John Hare, actor.

Odhams Press Ltd.   Photo : Maycock

TUNING IN TO "2LO"

Photo : Cen. Press

Sir Ernest Shackleton's expedition to the Antarctic, which set sail the previous year was never completed, as he died of heart failure early in 1922. He is here seen with Scouts Marr and Mooney, specially chosen to accompany the expedition.

On the last day of February the wedding took place between Princess Mary and Viscount Lascelles, son of the Earl of Harewood. This portrait was taken immediately after the wedding which was celebrated at Westminster Abbey.

The liner *Mauretania* set up in May a new record of 5 days 8 hours 56 minutes for the crossing from New York to Southampton. In November she broke this record by crossing from New York to Plymouth in 4 days, 23 hours, 15 minutes.

Photo: Topical

Ireland was torn by civil war once more this year over the signing of the Treaty that brought the Free State into being. The Four Courts in Dublin were seized and burned in April and the Extreme Nationalist revolt was not crushed till July, after much loss of life and property. *Above*: The scene at the Four Courts during the battle for their possession.

Photo : Topical

The opening of Dail Eireann, or Chamber of Deputies, of the Irish Free State Parliament on September 9 in Dublin. Mr. William Thomas Cosgrave was elected President. The building, Leinster House, was closely guarded, owing to the general disturbances, and, as in a fortress, the Government continued to operate under these conditions for nearly a year.

Photo : *Cen. Press*

Under the guidance of Mr. Cosgrave, who is here seen addressing a meeting, the Irish Free State began to settle down.

The post-war prosperity of 1918-20 had suddenly collapsed, and the now too-familiar problem of Unemployment wa
already beginning to loom large. Over a million men were unemployed, and there was considerable distress in the countr

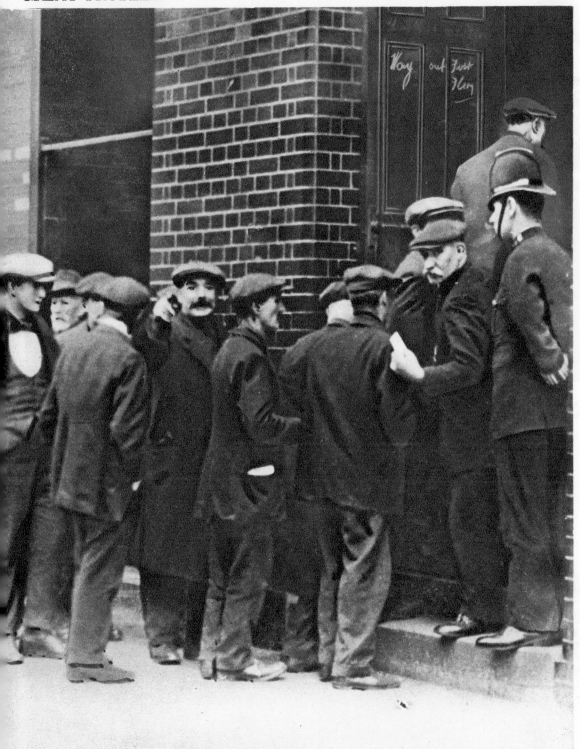

Above is seen a queue of men waiting outside a Labour Exchange to draw their Unemployment Insurance money. The question of unemployment has been one of the main problems of every government that has taken office since 1921.

Photo : S. & G.

On July 17, the King opened the new County Hall of the London County Council, situated on the south side of the River Thames, near Westminster Bridge. The picture above shows Their Majesties at the opening ceremony.

Photo : Topical

The County Hall. This picture, taken from the river, of the new headquarters of the L.C.C. shows the building as it is to-day.

Photo : *Topical*

The sports events of 1922 were exceptionally interesting. The victory of Lord Woolavington's *Captain Cuttle*, with Steve Donoghue up, in the Derby was extremely popular. Above is a photograph showing the thrilling finish of the race.

Photo : Topical

The increasing popularity of tennis made it imperative that more accommodation be allowed for spectators. The new stadium at Wimbledon was opened this year to take the place of the original All England Club premises in Worple Road.

Marie Lloyd one of the most popular comediennes of her time, died in October, and crowds thronged to her funeral. Among the very many well-known songs she sang was "One of the Ruins that Cromwell Knocked About a Bit."

Towards the end of October the Conservatives ceased to support the Coalition Government, and Mr. Lloyd George, who was at that time Premier, resigned. Mr. Bonar Law (shown in the above photograph) took office as Prime Minister, despite the fact that he was a very sick man, formed a Conservative Cabinet but resigned on May 20, 1923. The responsibilities of his office were thought to have hastened his death, which occurred on October 30, 1923.

"Toc H" is an organisation which had its foundation during the War, when the Rev. P. B. Clayton, M.C., organised a soldiers' club at Talbot House in Poperinghe. After the War, "Tubby" Clayton established a Talbot House Club in London, calling it "Toc H," and the Prince of Wales became patron. Above, the Prince is seen lighting the Lamp of Maintenance at the great mass meeting at Albert Hall. Leaning over the Prince is the Rev. P. B. Clayton.

PRINCIPAL EVENTS OF 1922

JAN. 5. Sir Ernest Shackleton dies on board the *Quest*.

,, 10. Duke of York inaugurates building of British Empire Exhibition, Wembley.

,, 12. Georges Carpentier knocks out George Cook, the Australian Champion.

,, 22. Death of Pope Benedict XV.

FEB. 3. Death of General Christian de Wet, famous Boer War leader.

,, 6. Cardinal Ratti, Archbishop of Milan, elected Pope Pius XI.
Washington Conference closes.

,, 14. International Court of Justice opens at the Hague.

,, 28. Princess Mary's marriage to Viscount Lascelles, K.G., at Westminster Abbey.

MAR. 1. Termination of British Protectorate over Egypt.

,, 16. Sultan of Egypt proclaimed King Fuad I.

,, 21. The Queen opens the new Waterloo Station.

,, 27. General C. G. Bruce's Everest Expedition leaves Darjeeling.

APR. 1. Cambridge wins Boat Race.

,, 7. Two aeroplanes London-Paris collide in France, 6 killed.

,, 13. Sir Ross Smith, the airman, killed at Brooklands.

,, 16. Treaty between Germany and U.S.S.R. signed at Genoa.

,, 23. Death of Lord Leopold Arthur Louis Mountbatten.

MAY 1. *Mauretania* sets up record, New York to Southampton, 5 days, 8 hours, 56 minutes.

,, 11. Kid Lewis knocked out by Georges Carpentier.

,, 13. Final Plenary Session of the Genoa Conference.

,, 15. Death of Sir Leslie Ward, "Spy" of *Punch*.

,, 20. P. & O. liner *Egypt* sunk off Ushant after collision with a French cargo boat. 87 lives lost.

,, 29. Minimum postage for letters reduced to 1½d.

MAY 31. Lord Woolavington wins Derby with Captain Cuttle.

JUNE 8. Marriage of King Alexander of Yugo-Slavia with Princess Marie of Rumania.

,, 16. Mount Everest expedition reaches 27,200 ft.

,, 22. Assassination of Field-Marshal Sir Henry Wilson in London.

JULY 17. King opens London County Council's new Hall.

AUG. 1. Death of Dr. Alexander Graham Bell, inventor of the telephone.

,, 12. Arthur Griffith, President of the Dail Eireann, dies suddenly.

,, 14. Death of Viscount Northcliffe.

,, 22. General Collins shot in ambush.

SEPT. 4. Death of G. R. Sims, journalist.

,, 9. First Irish Parliament under the Free State meets in Dublin.

OCT. 7. Death of Marie Lloyd, variety artiste.

,, 23. Mr. Bonar Law elected leader of Unionist Party and becomes Prime Minister.

,, 31. Death of Father Bernard Vaughan.

NOV. 5. Ex-Kaiser married to Princess Hermine of Reuss at Doorn.

,, 9. Attempt to murder Sir William Horwood, Commissioner of Metropolitan Police.

,, 14. Official beginning of broadcasting in this country.

,, 15. General Election. Conservative majority.

DEC. 4. Timothy Healy becomes Governor General of Southern Ireland.

,, 5. Irish Free State Constitution Bill receives Royal Assent.

,, 6. First Free State Parliament meets.

,, 12. Duke of Abercorn sworn in at Belfast as Governor of Northern Ireland.

Photograph of the massive Gold Mask of Tutankhamen by Mr. Harry Burton of the Metropolitan Museum of Art, New York. World copyright strictly reserved.

EXCAVATIONS IN THE TOMB OF TUTANKHAMEN

261

On the 26th of April, H.R.H. the Duke of York was married to Lady Elizabeth Bowes-Lyon, in Westminster Abbey.

A happy and informal photograph of the Duke and Duchess of York, taken walking together on their honeymoon.

The sports events of the early part of 1923 were more than usually interesting. Oxford won the Boat Race by three-quarters of a length. The picture shows the rival boats at Hammersmith. From 1924 onwards Cambridge enjoyed an unbroken series of victories unprecedented in the history of the race.

Photo : Topical

WEMBLEY'S

FIRST

CUP-FINAL

ON April 28 the Cup Final between Bolton Wanderers and West Ham United was played for the first time in the new Wembley Stadium. Bolton Wanderers won by 2 goals to nil. The crowds were so enormous that they broke down the barriers and the police had to form cordons to prevent spectators overflowing on to the ground. *Above*: the police endeavouring to keep the crowd back, and the lower picture shows Joe Smith (*right*), the Bolton Wanderers' captain, shaking hands with George Kay, captain of West Ham United, before the kick-off.

Photos: S. & G.

Jack Hobbs, the great English cricketer, on May 8 made his hundredth century in first-class cricket. Two years later he made his 126th century, thus equalling the record of W. G. Grace. Here is a picture of Jack Hobbs " in action."

Photo : Topical

Mr. Stanley Baldwin, who was Chancellor of the Exchequer, became Prime Minister for the first time following the resignation of Mr. Bonar Law on May 20. He is seen in the above photograph with his wife and daughter.

Photo : Marconi

Broadcasting in this year celebrated its first official birthday. Wireless programmes were broadcast from Savoy Hill
Here is a scene inside one of the studios of 2LO. The artists at the microphone are singing a duet.

The scene in the Lord Chancellor's office when the writs were issued for the General Election of this year

Photos : S. & G.

Wireless brought the election results into the homes of the people, enabling them to get the very latest results in the privacy and comfort of their own fireside. Here is a family group listening eagerly for the announcements.

PRINCIPAL EVENTS OF 1923

JAN. 1. 100 acres of Ken Wood Estate bought to extend Hampstead Heath.

,, 2-4. Reparations Conference.

,, 8. French troops occupy the Ruhr.

,, 10. Diamond Jubilee of Metropolitan Railway.

FEB. 1. French proclaim state of siege throughout the Ruhr.

,, 4. Turkey refuses to sign Peace Treaty.

,, 7. Princess Mary gives birth to a son.

,, 10. Death of Von Rontgen, discoverer of the X-ray.

,, 16. Sealed chamber of King Tutankhamen's at Luxor opened.

MAR. 24. Oxford wins Boat Race.

,, 26. Death of Sarah Bernhardt.

APR. 1. New Customs duties in force in Irish Free State.

,, 5. Death of Earl of Carnarvon, famous Egyptologist.

,, 19. Egyptian Constitution signed.

,, 26. Duke of York's marriage to Lady Elizabeth Bowes-Lyon.

,, 28. First Association Football Cup Final at Wembley—Bolton Wanderers 2; West Ham 0.

MAY 8. Jack Hobbs scores 100th century in first-class cricket.

,, 14. Crash of London-Paris aeroplane. 6 killed.

,, 20. Bonar Law resigns.

,, 22-28. Mr. Stanley Baldwin forms Ministry.

JUNE 4. S.S. *Trevassa* founders in Indian Ocean.

,, 6. Mr. B. Irish's Papyrus wins Derby.

,, 10. Death of Pierre Loti (Capt. Julien Viaud), French writer.

,, 16. Submarine XI, largest under-water craft in the world, launched at Chatham.

,, 25. Seventh International Air Congress (first to be held in London).

JULY 10. Death of Albert Chevalier, actor.

,, 17. Lausanne Conference ends.

,, 24. Peace Treaty with Turkey signed at Lausanne.

,, 30. Death of Sir Charles Hawtrey, actor.

AUG. 2. Death of Warren G. Harding, President, U.S.A.

,, 15. De Valera arrested by Free State troops.

SEPT. 1. Earthquake in Japan destroys Yokohama and most of Tokio.

,, 6. Prince of Wales sails for Canada.

,, 10. Irish Free State admitted to League of Nations.

,, 12. Southern Rhodesia incorporated in British Empire.

,, 13. Army revolt in Spain.

,, 14. Disaster to London-Manchester Air Mail.

,, 16. Fall of Spanish Cabinet and appointment of military directorate.

,, 23. Death of Viscount Morley.

,, 26. Miss Margaret Bondfield elected first woman chairman of General Council of Trades Union Congress.

OCT. 1. Imperial Conference opens. Southern Rhodesia becomes self-governing colony.

,, 2. Allied troops evacuate Constantinople. Imperial Economic Conference opens.

,, 20. Prince of Wales arrives home from Canada.

,, 30. Turkey declared Republic. Death of Andrew Bonar Law.

NOV. 8. Imperial Conference ends.

,, 9. Premier's speech at Lord Mayor's Banquet, Guildhall, broadcast for first time.

DEC. 6. General Election Polling Day.

,, 27. Death of Alexandre Gustave Eiffel, designer of the famous tower in Paris.

Photo : " Times"

THE HISTORIC CHANGE AT 10 DOWNING STREET

Photo : Topical

An unconventional study of Mr. Ramsay MacDonald, first Labour Prime Minister, seen here with his daughter, Sheila. The photograph was taken in the grounds at Chequers, the official country residence of Britain's Prime Minister.

Photo : S. & G.

Above is a group of the new Labour Cabinet Ministers leaving Buckingham Palace after having "kissed hands." Reading from left to right are Mr. J. H. Thomas, Mr. Ramsay MacDonald, Mr. J. R. Clynes, and Mr. Arthur Henderson.

Photo : Topical

The barriers seen above were erected at the head of Downing Street but were ultimately removed early this year. They were originally placed there as a precautionary measure against trouble arising as a result of political unrest.

Front row, seated from left to right : Mr. William Adamson, Lord Parmoor, Mr. Philip Snov
Second row : Mr. C. P. Trevelyan, Mr. Stephen Walsh, Lord Thomson, Lord Chelmsford, Lord O.
Back row : Mr. Sidney V

Photo : Elliott and Fry

Haldane, Mr. Ramsay MacDonald, Mr. J. R. Clynes, Mr. J. H. Thomas, Mr. Arthur Henderson,
E. Noel-Buxton, Mr. Josiah Wedgwood, Mr. Vernon Hartshorn, and Mr. Tom Shaw,
ohn Wheatley, Mr. F. W. Jowett.

The British Empire Exhibition at Wembley was formally opened on April 23 of this year by His Majesty the King.

Photo : Cen. Press

The above picture shows the Royal Coach amidst the ceremonial scene in the huge Stadium on the opening day.

ALL THE FUN OF THE FAIR!

The British Empire Exhibition at Wembley in the height of its first season. Quite a large area of the grounds was devoted to an Amusement Park. Here is shown the Scenic Railway—one of the most popular of amusements.

The photograph shows the central part of the Exhibition ground which was laid out with flower beds, with a big central lake for boating. The ornamental water-fall made an attractive setting against the white walls of the pavilions.

Lord Derby, whose family had instituted the famous race, won the Blue Riband of the Turf this year with " Sansovino."
A Derby had not won the Derby for over one hundred years.   Lord Derby is shown above leading in the winner.

Photo : Cen. Press

A striking photograph of the King, showing him at the wheel of his yacht, *Britannia*, during the Cowes Regatta week.

Photo : " Times "

July 19 witnessed the impressive ceremony of the consecration of the unfinished Cathedral at Liverpool before a large assembly.

Photo : " Daily Herald "

The long projected plan of exploring the coal seams that were known to exist in certain parts of Kent came to fruition this year. The photograph shows the first load being brought to the surface at Bettshanger Colliery, near Dover.

The enormous and complicated task of rebuilding the Bank of England was started in this year. Some regret was felt by lovers of Old London that parts of the original structure had to be demolished. Above is the little-known garden court.

Photos : Humphrey and Vera Joel

One of the most interesting rooms in the original Bank of England building was the famous court-room with its spacious and dignified design. The picture shows the room as it appeared before the commencement of the rebuilding.

PRINCIPAL EVENTS OF 1924

JAN. 7. Direct communication by transatlantic cable and land wire opened by Western Union Telegraph Company between London and Chicago.

,, 21. Death of Lenin.

22. Ramsay MacDonald becomes Prime Minister of the first Labour Government.

,, 26. Earl of Athlone opens South African Parliament.

FEB. 1. Great Britain recognises U.S.S.R.

,, 3. Death of Dr. Woodrow Wilson.

MAR. 25. King George of Greece deposed.

,, 29. Death of Sir Charles Stanford, composer.

APR. 21. Death of Eleanor Duse.
Death of Marie Corelli, Novelist.

,, 23. The King, accompanied by the Queen, opens British Empire Exhibition at Wembley.

,, 24. Train ferry service between Harwich and Zeebrugge opened by Prince George.

,, 26. Cup Tie Final at Wembley, Newcastle United 2; Aston Villa, 0.

MAY 11. Waterloo Bridge closed for repairs.

,, 12. King and Queen of Rumania arrive in London on state visit.

,, 18. Death of Major-General Sir Charles Townshend.

,, 25. King and Queen present at Empire Thanksgiving Service at Wembley, which was broadcast.

,, 26. King and Queen of Italy arrive in London.

,, 29. Death of Paul Cambon, former French Ambassador to Great Britain.

JUNE 4. Lord Derby wins the Derby with Sansovino. First time for 137 years holder of Derby title won this race founded by his family.

,, 22. King and Queen of Denmark arrive in London.

JULY 11. E. H. Liddell (Great Britain) won final heat of 400 metres in Olympic Games, in 47.3/5ths secs.

,, 16. Reparations Conference opens in London.

,, 19. King and Queen attend consecration of new Liverpool Cathedral.

AUG. 3. Death of Joseph Conrad.

,, 8. Treaties between England and U.S.S.R. signed.

,, 21. Princess Mary gives birth to second son.

,, 23. Prince of Wales leaves for U.S.A. and Canada.

SEP. 23. Lieuts. Smith and Nelson complete the world flight at Santa Monica.

OCT. 8. Government defeated.

,, 9. Dissolution of Parliament announced by Premier.

,, 11. First appointment of Labour Governor, Mr. James O'Grady, for Tasmania.

,, 13. Death of Anatole France.

,, 29. France recognises the U.S.S.R.
General Election. Labour defeated. Death of Frances Hodgson Burnett, author.

,, 31. Prince of Wales returned from tour of U.S.A. and Canada.

NOV. 6. Mr. Stanley Baldwin's Cabinet announced.

,, 29. Death of Giacomo Puccini, composer.

DEC. 1. A woman barrister appears as an advocate in the Court of Criminal Appeal for the first time.

,, 7. Death of Gene Stratton Porter, authoress.

Photo : Cen. Press

IN THIS YEAR THE QUEEN MOTHER DIED.

Before the War a report had been issued that the Dome of St. Paul's Cathedral showed signs of cracking.   In this year an appeal for funds was made.   The appeal organisation was aided very greatly by The Dean, the Very Rev. W. R. Inge.

Photo : Topical

One of London's most famous landmarks—the Statue of Eros—was removed from its site, Piccadilly Circus, in April during the reconstruction of the Underground Railway station. The statue was not replaced for several years.

On March 18 a disastrous fire broke out at Madame Tussaud's Waxwork Exhibition and destroyed the entire col

Photo : G.P.U.

its. Many valuable Napoleonic relics were also lost. Here is a view of the firemen playing their hoses on the building.

Photo : S. & G.

The British Empire Exhibition, Wembley, was re-opened with great ceremony by the King and Queen on May 9.

Photo : S. & G.

In contrast to the pageantry of the opening is this picture of Their Majesties making a trip on the model railway.

This year commemorated the centenary of the first railway built between Stockton and Darlington, opened on September 27, 1825. The centenary was celebrated by a pageant in which an old engine (seen above) was driven slowly past interested spectators. Below, a powerful 1925 British engine clearly marks the progress made in one hundred years.

Photos: S. & G.

AN interesting experiment was successfully carried out in October in the launching of aeroplanes from the R.33 while in flight. An aeroplane which has just been launched from the R.33 can be seen on the left.

Photo: S. & G.

H.M. Queen Alexandra, the Queen Mother, died on November 20, at Sandringham, the Royal residence

in Norfolk. Above is a view, taken from the air, of the house and part of the grounds.

Photo : Topical.

Lying-in-state of Queen Alexandra in Westminster Abbey, where the public came to pay a last loving tribute.

Photo : S. & G.

The funeral of the Queen Mother passing through the snow-covered streets of London on its way to Windsor where the Queen was buried beside her husband, Edward VII. The King is seen above, leading the procession of mourners.

Photo : S. & G.

British troops began to leave Cologne on November 30—a detachment marching out of the city in a blinding snowstorm.

Photo: S. & G.

Seven European nations—Germany, Belgium, France, Great Britain, Italy, Poland, and Czechoslovakia—met at Locarno to discuss methods of ensuring the peace in Europe. The terms of the agreement were initialled by the delegates of the Powers at Locarno on October 16, and the Pact was finally signed at the Foreign Office in London on December 1.

PRINCIPAL EVENTS OF 1925

JAN. 1. Viscount Jellicoe made Earl Brocars of Southampton.

,, 26. Mr. Alan Cobham made a successful flight over the Himalayas.

MAR. 18. Fire destroys Madame Tussaud's waxwork exhibition.

,, 19. King and Queen left London to cruise in the Mediterranean.

,, 20. Death of the Marquess Curzon of Kedleston, English statesman, aged 66.

,, 25. Prince Henry opened London-Southend road.

,, 28. Cambridge wins the boat race.
Prince of Wales left for British West Africa, South Africa, and South America.
Death of Lord Rawlinson.

APR. 14. Death of John Singer Sargent, R.A., English artist.

,, 25. Sheffield United beat Cardiff City in Cup Tie Final. (1-0).

,, 26. Hindenburgh elected President of German Republic.

MAY 7. Death of Viscount Leverhulme.

,, 11. Direct telephone communication between Rome and London established for the first time.

,, 13. Death of Viscount Milner, British statesman.

,, 14. Death of Sir Rider Haggard, British novelist born in 1856.

,, 22. Death of the Earl of Ypres, English soldier.

,, 27. Mr. H. E. Morriss's Manna won the Derby.

MAY 30. The King opens the Great West Road at Brentford.

JUN. 9. The King and Queen open new buildings of Bristol University.

,, 29. The King and Queen open Canadian Government Buildings in Trafalgar Square.

JULY 1. Railway Centenary Exhibition.

,, 4. Captain Barnard wins King's Cup Air Race.

,, 18. The King opens Ken Wood for the use of the general public.

OCT. 13. Successful vertical ascent and descent at Farnborough in Spanish helicopter. (Captain Courtenay.)

,, 15. Return of the Prince of Wales from his tour in Africa and South America.

,, 26. U.S.A. retains Schneider Cup.

,, 30. Rt. Hon. Edward Wood appointed Viceroy of India in succession to Lord Reading.

NOV. 2. New electric railway from Baker Street to Watford opened.

,, 16. Mr. Alan Cobham starts flight to South Africa.

,, 20. Death of H.M. Queen Alexandra.

,, 27. Funeral of Queen Alexandra.

DEC. 1. Locarno Treaty signed at the Foreign Office.
British troops evacuate Cologne.

,, 3. Agreement reached between Great Britain, Irish Free State and Northern Ireland on the Boundary Question.

,, 16. Princess Mary inaugurated the work of constructing the Mersey Tunnel.

NO NEWSPAPERS! THE PUBLIC ANXIOUS FOR NEWS!

Photo : Topical.

On March 6 the Shakespeare Memorial Theatre at Stratford-on-Avon was almost entirely destroyed by fire. The picture shows the flaming roof and tower. Shakespeare lovers from all over the world have made their pilgrimage to see Shakespeare's plays performed at this theatre. A fund was opened and eventually a new theatre was built on the site.

Photo : S. & G.

Mr. Alan Cobham (*inset*) arrived at Croydon on March 13, after his first spectacular flight to and from the Cape.   On June 30 he set out once more—this time to fly to Australia and back, a distance of 28,000 miles.   His seaplane is seen just before landing on the Thames beside the Houses of Parliament on October 1.   He received a knighthood on October 6.

Photo : Central Press.

On April 21, the Duchess of York gave birth to a daughter—Princess Elizabeth, the first grand-daughter of the Queen

This picture shows the actual scene at the switchboard when London this year spoke to America by radio telephone.

Photo : Topical.

At the end of April, the Government subsidy to the mining industry ceased, and as the miners refused to accept reduced wages, work in the mines stopped altogether. · The picture below shows a typical scene of activity at a pit head before the strike began, and, above, the line of empty trucks in a siding, symbolic of the complete deadlock which had now arisen.

Photo: Central Press.

The dispute dragged on until nearly the end of November.
Miners fill in their leisure time with a game of cards.

Photo : Central Press.

After last-minute negotiations had broken down, the General Council of the Trades Union Congress, with the authority of the unions, called a National Strike to start at midnight on May 3, in support of the miners. In response, industrial workers throughout the country ceased work, all vital services being affected. *Above:* Volunteers offering their services.

Photos : Topical.

Emergency powers were immediately assumed by the Government. Mounted police are here guarding a tramway depot.

On May 4, services were practically at a standstill. Above is an armoured car acting as a convoy to Food Lorries. Special measures were taken with regard to food supplies. A label " Food Only " can just be discerned on the front of leading lorry. This was respected by the strikers, who strongly criticised the Governments demonstration of military force.

Photos : Topical.

Large numbers of amateurs volunteered to drive buses and trams.   The first volunteer-driven bus sets off on its journey.

Hyde Park was closed to the public, and used as a food depot. Lines of milk churns awaiting distribution.

Photo : Topical.

MORE
NATIONAL STRIKE
MEMORIES

Right : Special Constables who have just enrolled, receiving instructions as to their duties. *Below :* Naval ratings manning an important power station.

Photos : *Topical.*

Photo: S. & G.

To simplify the congestion of traffic in the main London thoroughfares, the " roundabout " system was instituted. **The** picture shows the new system in operation at Piccadilly, which at that time was undergoing many structural alterations. Apart from the new buildings in course of erection, a great new Underground station was then being constructed.

Photos : S. & G.

Miss Gertrude Ederle, the young American swimmer, was the first woman to swim the Channel. She also established a new record by swimming from France to England on August 6 in 14 hours 31 minutes, thus beating the previous record by about two hours. She is seen above in the water and, below, receiving advice from Mr. Jabez Wolff, her trainer.

Photo : Topical.

During 1926, England wrested the Ashes from Australia. Above, the enthusiastic crowd swarming across the ground to congratulate the English team. The first four matches were drawn—England winning the fifth game at the Oval.

From the film, "The Sheik."

On August 23 died Rudolph Valentino, film star, who captured the public imagination to a remarkable degree. He is seen here in one of his best-known pictures, *The Sheik*. Valentino cast an extraordinary spell over the women of his time.

313

Photo: Topical

WONDERFUL WIMBLEDON

AT Wimbledon this year was celebrated the Jubilee of the lawn tennis championship meeting. *Above:* the King and Queen watch the game, the Queen wearing smoked glasses to protect her eyes from the sun's glare. *Below:* Jean Borotra in play. It was this famous champion who set the fashion of wearing a beret; women have found this form of headgear one of the most comfortable in existence.

The 1925 Nobel Prize for Literature was awarded this year to George Bernard Shaw

Photo : Yevonde.

PRINCIPAL EVENTS OF 1926

JAN. 4. Death of Queen Margherita of Italy.

,, 21. Lord Lloyd, High Commissioner of Egypt, opens the Sennar Dam.

,, 31. Evacuation of Cologne by the British troops.

FEB. 17. Alan Cobham reaches the Cape, after flight of 8,000 miles.

MAR. 6. Shakespeare Memorial Theatre at Stratford-on-Avon burnt down.

,, 13. Alan Cobham lands at Croydon, concluding a flight of 16,000 miles from London to Capetown and back.

,, 20. Death of Louise Josephine Eugenie, Dowager Queen of Denmark.

,, 27. Cambridge win the Boat Race.

,, 29. C.O.D. parcel service came into operation.

APR. 3. Lord Irwin took office as Viceroy of India.

,, 19. Death of Sir Squire Bancroft—actor-manager.

,, 21. Birth of a daughter to Duchess of York (Princess Elizabeth).

,, 24. Russo-German Treaty signed.
,, Bolton Wanderers beat Manchester City in Cup Tie Final (1—0).

,, 30. Stoppage of work in coal mines.

MAY 3. National Strike Begins.

,, 9. Commander Byrd and Floyd Bennett fly over North Pole.

,, 12. National Strike Ends.

,, 14. General Pilsudski captures Warsaw.

,, 16. Amundsen in " Norge " lands after crossing North Pole.

JUNE 2. Lord Woolavington wins Derby with Coronach.

,, 4. French Senate ratifies Locarno Pact.

,, 24. Jubilee of the telephone.

,, 30. Alan Cobham leaves for Australia and back.

JULY 2. Death of Emile Coué, auto-suggestionist.

,, 12. Caillaux and Churchill sign an agreement for funding of French War Debt.

AUG. 1. Death of Izrael Zangwill, Jewish author.

,, Death of Desire Joseph Mercer, Belgian Prelate.

,, 6. Miss Gertrude Ederle of New York, first woman to swim channel. Also beat fastest time by two hours.

,, 15. Alan Cobham arrives at Melbourne.

,, 18. England wins final Test Match of the season at the Oval, wresting championship from Australia.

,, 23. Rudolph Valentino dies.

SEPT. 10. German delegates at League of Nations.

,, 11. Spain announces withdrawal from League of Nations.

OCT. 1. Alan Cobham returns to London after a flight to Australia and back.

,, 2. French air liner from Paris to London wrecked near Penshurst.

,, 14. Lord Oxford and Asquith resigns leadership of Liberal Party.

,, 19. Imperial Conference at Downing Street.

,, 24. Commander Kenworthy joins Labour Party.

NOV. 1. Betting Tax comes into operation.

,, 4. Crown Prince Leopold of Belgium marries Princess Astrid of Sweden at Stockholm.

,, 15. House of Commons gives approval to scheme for replacing British Broadcasting Company by a public corporation.

FIRST AUTOMATIC TELEPHONE EXCHANGE OPENED AT HOLBORN.

The Duke and Duchess of York left England on January 6 to open the Parliament Building

Photo: S. & G.

Australia's new Capital, Canberra. The picture shows the opening ceremony on May 9.

The upper picture shows work in progress during the preparation of the foundations of Canberra in 1920. Below is a view of one of the many extensive Government Buildings in the magnificent new capital of the Commonwealth.

Photos: " Daily Herald"

Photo: Topical.

The situation in China in the early part of the year was beginning seriously to threaten British life and property in Shanghai, and the Government dispatched a contingent of troops to the Far East. They are here seen embarking.

Photo: Topical.

An attempt to bring a revised version of the Prayer Book into use aroused great controversy throughout the country. Many who had protested against it marched in procession to Lambeth Palace, where they are seen here outside the gates.

EPIC
OF THE
ATLANTIC

CHARLES LINDBERGH, a young American aviator, was the first man to fly the Atlantic alone. He received a tremendous reception both in Paris—where he landed at 10 p.m. on May 21, at the conclusion of his flight—and also later in London. He is seen above being congratulated on his arrival in France by a famous French aviator Rene Fonck, and below arriving at Croydon in his 'plane *Spirit of St. Louis.*

Photos: S. & G. and " Flight."

Greyhound Racing was launched in London at the White City on June 20. The picture shows the meeting in progress.

Photo: Topical.

Photo : " Times"

L.N.E.R. inaugurated a non-stop run between King's Cross and Newcastle on July 11.   This marked another stage of Britain's bid for world supremacy in railways. Here is the *Flying Scotsman* making the now famous non-stop journey.

Photo: Topical.

In July of this year the L.G.O. Co. was granted permission to run their passenger services past Buckingham Palace. This was also the year in which the now familiar covered-top buses generally replaced the old "open" top vehicles.

Field-Marshal Lord Plumer unveiled the Menin Gate on July 24, as a memorial to the British Armies who fought at Ypres.

Photo: Cen. Press.

Photo: Cen. Press.

The memorial contains the names of nearly 60,000 officers and men who fell in the Salient and who lie in unknown graves.

——— PRINCIPAL EVENTS OF 1927 ———

JAN. 6. Duke and Duchess of York leave for Australia.

,, 7. Wireless telephonic service between London and New York inaugurated.

,, 18. New Parliament Building at Delhi opened by the Viceroy.

FEB. 7. New prayer book published.

,, 24. Death of Sir Edward Marshall-Hall, K.C.

MAR. 7. Earthquake in Japan.

APR. 2. Cambridge win Boat Race.

,, 23. Cup Final at Wembley: Cardiff City 1, Arsenal 0.

MAY 4. Economic Conference opened at Geneva; U.S.S.R. represented.

,, 9. Duke of York opens Parliament at Canberra.

,, 20. Capt. Charles Lindberg leaves New York to fly to Paris.

,, 21. Capt. Lindberg arrives in Paris in 33½ hours.

,, 22. R.A.F. flight from Cairo—Cape and back successfully.

,, 27. Britain severs diplomatic relations with U.S.S.R.

JUNE 1. Mr. Frank Curzon's Call Boy wins the Derby.

,, 2. European and U.S.A. troops arrive in Pekin and Tientsin.

,, 6. Transatlantic flight by Clarence Chamberlin, and Mr. Levine as passenger.

,, 14. Death of Jerome K. Jerome, author.

,, 20. Greyhound racing commenced at the White City.

,, 27. Return of Duke and Duchess of York from Australian tour.

JULY 19. The King and Queen opened new Gladstone Docks on the Mersey, Liverpool.

,, 20. Death of ex-King Ferdinand of Rumania.

,, 24. Field-Marshal Lord Plumer unveils war memorial at Menin Gate.

AUG. 4. Death of John Dillon, Irish leader.

SEPT. 14. Death of Arthur Bourchier, actor-manager.

,, 26. Flight-Lieut. Webster wins Schneider Cup for Britain at Venice, at an average speed of 281 m.p.h.

OCT. 13. Death of William le Quex, novelist.

NOV. 12. First automatic telephone service in London at Holborn Exchange.

DEC. 15. House of Commons defeats New Prayer Book.

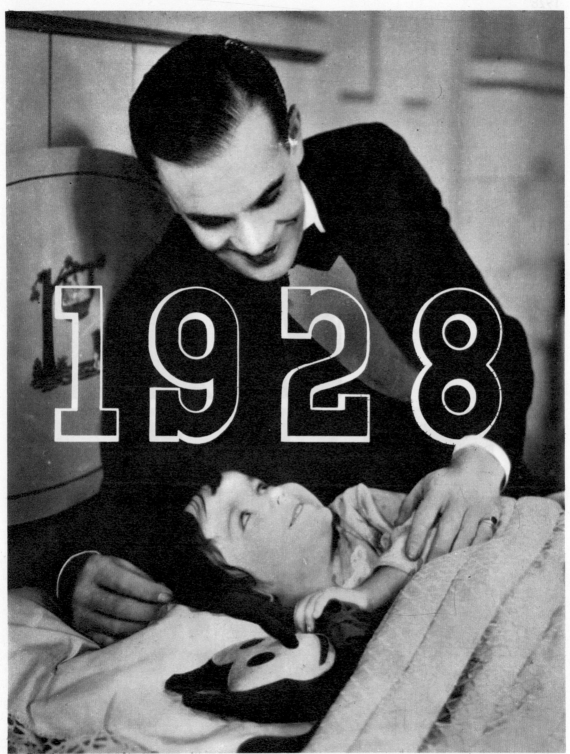

From the film, " Sonny Boy."

COMING OF THE " TALKIES "

OBITUARY— THOMAS HARDY EARL HAIG

EARLY in the year, Great Britain lost two famous men.

Right : Thomas Hardy, O.M., the world-famous novelist and author of "Tess of the D'Urbervilles," who died on January 11 at the age of 87. His ashes lie in Westminster Abbey.

Earl Haig, the Commander-in-Chief of the British Armies in France during the Great War, died on January 29, aged 66. Below : His coffin, covered with a Union Jack and with a wreath of Flanders poppies laid on it, is here seen being carried from the house where he died. He was buried at Dryburgh Abbey, Scotland.

Photo: S. & G.

The Indian Commission

ON February 3 the Indian Commission, headed by Sir John Simon, landed in Bombay to inquire into the problems of government in India. The members of the commission, seen below with Sir John Simon at the head of the table, first toured the country gathering information then returned to England in the spring. In the autumn they went out again to India, to begin their public sittings. The picture on the right shows Sir John Simon being welcomed on his return to England.

Photo : Topical.

Photos: S. & G.

The worst Thames flood within living memory occurred early in the year. Here is seen the unusual sight of the Tower moat—ordinarily used as a football ground—filled with water. At other parts of the river there was great devastation.

Photos: S. & G.

The seriousness of the floods was not fully realised until the Embankment at Westminster gave way. Fourteen people were drowned as they slept in basements near the river and much damage was done to the surrounding property.

TOILERS
OF THE
SEA

ON February 13 the Prince of Wales was appointed Master of the Merchant Navy and Fishing Fleets. The two pictures on this page portray the activities of the North Sea fishermen. The lower picture is of a typical trawler scene on a misty day at sea and, left, a representative member of the North Sea Fishing Fleet.

Photos: D. Herald.

Photo: Topical.

DEATH
OF THE
EARL of OXFORD

THE Earl of Oxford and Asquith, Liberal Prime Minister for many years and Premier at the outbreak of the Great War, died on February 15, at the age of 75. He was buried in the country churchyard of All Saints Church, Sutton Courtney, Oxfordshire. Many famous people attended the funeral and paid their tribute at the simple graveside service.

Photo: S. & G.

1928

15½ DAYS TO AUSTRALIA !

IN February Mr. Bert Hinkler (inset) made a record flight from England to Australia, reaching Port Darwin on February 22, 15½ days after leaving England. The picture shows his arrival at Sydney amidst a number of welcoming planes. His 'plane bears the letters G.E.B.O.V. Later, in 1933 he set out on a flight to endeavour to beat the existing London to Australia record. His fate was not known until April 28 of that year when his body and the crashed 'plane were discovered in Tuscany.

Photos: S. & G. and " Flight."

Photo: S. & G.

On May 19 the foundations of the new building for the Parliament of Northern Ireland were laid by the Governor, the Duke of Abercorn. The scene in the photograph shows the crowds and soldiers in the beautiful Stormont Castle Park.

NORTH POLE TRAGEDY

ON May 24 the famous Italian explorer, General Nobile, flew over the North Pole in the airship, *Italia*. On the next day the airship crashed. Roald Amundsen, the Polar explorer, lost his life while attempting to fly to the rescue of the crew. The top picture shows the *Italia* in flight and, on right, General Nobile.

Photos: S. & G. and Topical.

Gainsborough Pictures

A scene during the production of *The City of Play*, one of the Gainsborough Studios early talkies. A very primitive affair when compared with the elaborate paraphernalia now used in the modern Studios. Notice the "mike" above actor's head.

Miss Amelia Earhart achieved the distinction of being the first woman to cross the Atlantic by air.   She flew as a passenger with Messrs. Gordon and Stultz, arriving in England on June 18 after a journey from Newfoundland of 22 hours.

Photos: S. & G.

A great sea tragedy occurred in November when the British liner *Vestris* sank, with a loss of 115 lives.   This dramatic picture shows lifebelts attached to lifelines being thrown from a rescue ship to survivors struggling for life in the water.

Croydon Aerodrome in its modern form was re-opened by Lady Maud Hoare, wife of the Secretary of State for Air, on May 2. Above is a general view of the air-port, which is Britain's busiest air travel centre, with (below) a view of a wireless transmission room, whence contacts can be made with pilots in the air as to direction and weather conditions.

FACT TO OUTLAW WAR

Photos: " Flight."

A general view of the wireless control tower at Croydon—a nerve centre of the skyways—where elaborate electrical devices are used to regulate the movements of arriving and departing aeroplanes. Inset: The equipment in the cockpit of an aeroplane that enables the airman whilst in flight to communicate by wireless with the air-ports.

The " Kellogg Pact " (" The Pact of Paris ") was signed at Paris on August 27 by the representatives of fifteen nations. Mr. Kellogg, the American statesman, seen above, who was mainly responsible for the framing of that pact, was awarded the Nobel Peace Prize in 1930. By the treaty the countries agreed to outlaw war as a solution of international difficulties.

THE KING HAS HAD SOME SLEEP.
THE LOCAL CONDITION IS SATISFACTORY.
THE WEAKNESS AND TOXAEMIA ARE
CONSIDERABLE, BUT THE PULSE IS
STEADY AND HIS MAJESTY IS
NOT LOSING GROUND.

(SIGNED) STANLEY HEWETT,
HUGH M. RIGBY,
DAWSON OF PENN.

10.45 A.M.
13TH DECEMBER, 1928.

The King contracted a chill while attending the Armistice
Day Service and in the early part of December his condition gave rise to anxiety. Above, is the anxious crowd
reading the bulletin (inset) posted at the Palace gates.

Photo: S. & G.

PRINCIPAL EVENTS OF 1928

JAN. 11. Death of Thomas Hardy.

„ 27. Four R.A.F. flying boats reach India after 9,000 mile flight.

„ 29. Death of Earl Haig.

FEB. 3. Simon Commission lands in India.

„ 13. Prince of Wales appointed Master of the Merchant Navy and Fishing Fleets.

„ 15. Death of Lord Oxford and Asquith.

„ 22. Bert Hinkler flies from England to Port Darwin in 15½ days.

MAR. 22. Spain returns to the League.

„ 29. Death of Viscount Cave, Lord High Chancellor.

„ 31. Cambridge wins the Boat Race.

APR. 5. Mercedes Gleitze swims Straits of Gibraltar.

„ 10. Death of Stanley Weyman, novelist.

„ 12. Fitzmaurice, Koehl and von Huenefeld fly Atlantic, east to west.

„ 14. Simon Commission returns from India.

„ 21. Cup Tie Final, Wembley : Blackburn Rovers 3, Huddersfield Town 1.

MAY 1. Longest regular non-stop railway service in the world between King's Cross and Edinburgh (392½ miles) commenced by L.N.E.R.
Death of Sir Ebenezer Howard, founder of town planning movement.

„ 2. Croydon airport opened.

„ 16. Death of Sir Edmund Gosse, literary critic.
Prince of Wales opens Royal Tweed Bridge, Berwick.
New T.U.C. Headquarters opened by Ramsay MacDonald.

„ 17. Lady Heath arrives in England after her flight from the Cape.

„ 19. Foundations of new Parliament House for Northern Ireland laid by the Governor, the Duke of Abercorn.

„ 24. General Nobile flies over the North Pole in airship, *Italia*.

„ 31. Sir Alan Cobham returns to England after his survey flight round Africa.

JUNE 6. Sir H. Cunliffe Owen's Felstead wins the Derby.

„ 10. Airship *Italia* crashes.

„ 14. Death of Mrs. E. Pankhurst, pioneer of Women's Suffrage.

„ 18. Gertrude Earhart and companions fly from Newfoundland to England in 22 hours.
Death of Capt. Roald Amundsen.

„ 24. General Nobile rescued.

JULY 21. Death of Dame Ellen Terry.

AUG. 14. First motor coach service in Europe to provide sleeping bunks, put into operation between London and Liverpool.

„ 18. Death of Sir George Trevelyan, historian.

„ 19. Death of Viscount Haldane.

„ 27. Peace Pact signed in Paris.

SEPT. 6. Prince of Wales and Duke of Gloucester left England to tour East Africa.
Russia signs the Peace Pact.

OCT. 10. King and Queen open new Tyne Bridge.

„ 15. Graf Zeppelin reaches U.S.A. from Friedrichshafen, and returns.

„ 17. Death of Sir Francis Bernard Dicksee, President of Royal Academy.

NOV. 12. British liner *Vestris* founders with loss of 115 lives.

„ 21. Indisposition of the King. First bulletin issued.

DEC. 4. Owing to King's illness six councillors of State appointed. Queen, Prince of Wales, Duke of York, Archbishop of Canterbury, Lord Chancellor and Prime Minister.

„ 11. Prince of Wales returns home after lightning journey from Africa.

„ 20. Gas explosion in Holborn. £50,000 damage.

REPARATIONS

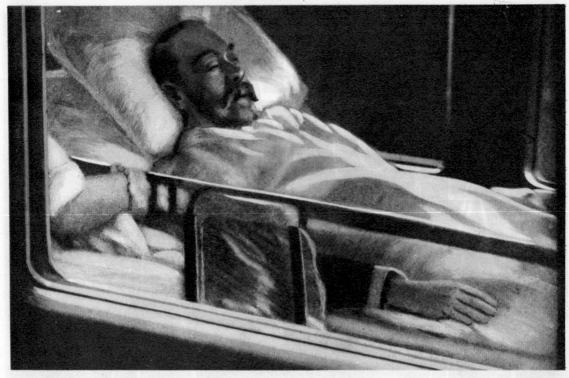

Photo: Topical.

On February 9 the King was sufficiently recovered from the serious illness which he contracted the previous year to be removed to Craigweil House, near Bognor, where he stayed, accompanied by the Queen and his nurses, during the first period of his convalescence. Above is seen the special ambulance in which he was transported to Bognor, now Bognor Regis.

Photo: S. & G.

This picture shows the King acknowledging the greetings of the people as he leaves Bognor, almost fully restored to health.

Photo: Cen. Press.

The King and Queen photographed in the grounds of Craigweil House, Bognor, during His Majesty's convalescence.

This double page picture shows an interesting aerial view of Windsor Castle, one of the most picturesque of t

Photo: Aero Films.

ng's residences.   It was here that His Majesty spent the latter part of May making his final recovery to health.

April 14 marked an advance in the history of aerial transport when the first Indian Air Mail arrived at Croydon.

Photo: S. & G.

The Metropolitan Police Force this year celebrated the centenary of its establishment by Sir Robert Peel on May 25. A large and representative force of London Police assembled in Hyde Park, there to be reviewed by the Prince of Wales.

Photo: Central Press.

On June 16 died General Bramwell Booth, son of the founder of the Salvation Army.   Here is a charming picture of him with his two grandchildren.   His unsparing devotion to the Army's work won him the affection and respect of millions.

"Weekly Illustrated" Photo: (Jarché)

The largest Scout Rally, or Jamboree, ever organised was opened at Arrowe Park, near Birkenhead, on July 30. Sir Robert Baden-Powell, the founder of the movement, received a barony on August 2 for the great work he had done for youth of Great Britain and the whole world. Above is a recent portrait of Lord Baden-Powell which was taken at his home.

Photos: S. & G.

The top picture shows the Prince of Wales, in Scout uniform, escorted by the Chief Scout, paying a welcome visit to the encampment in Arrowe Park.   50,000 Scouts of all nations had gathered for the Jamboree.   Above is seen a cheerful group of brother Scouts from many lands. This jamboree was a striking proof of the international strength of the Scout movement.

The General Election of 1929 was known—somewhat inaccurately—as the Flapper Election. Every woman over twenty-one was, for the first time, entitled to make use of her recently acquired privilege of voting, and women's votes greatly outnumbered those of the men. The Labour Party took office for the second time, with Mr. Ramsay MacDonald as Premier. Miss Margaret Bondfield was appointed Minister of Labour—the first woman to hold a Cabinet position.

Photos: S. & G.

Britain at this time was experimenting in the development of rigid airships. In the autumn, R101, the largest British airship yet built, was successfully launched. She is seen here leaving the mooring mast to undergo one of her test flights.

The financial sensation of this year was the Hatry crash, which affected large numbers of people whose money had been involved in his enterprises. Clarence Hatry stood his trial at the Old Bailey and ultimately received a heavy sentence. The case caused a good deal of public interest and despite its technical nature, queues lined up outside the Central Criminal Court every day in the hope of gaining admisson, and being able to hear the evidence for and against the accused man.

While Britain was experimenting along similar lines, Germany's Graf Zeppelin held supreme place as the world's

most successful airship and made a remarkable round-the-world flight.   She is seen here during a visit to this country.

Photo: *Central Press.*

During the year the Prince of Wales, in order to gain first-hand knowledge of the prevailing conditions in the coal mining industry, made tours of the distressed areas. He is here seen at the house of a Durham miner during one of his visits.

Odhams Press Ltd. Photo: Maycock.

During the Reparations Conference at the Hague, where revised financial proposals known as the Young Plan were discussed, Philip Snowden, who at the time was Chancellor of the Exchequer, ably defended the interests of Great Britain.

Mr. Arthur Henderson, as Secretary of State for Foreign Affairs, was largely responsible for the evacuation of the Rhineland by the Allied troops five years before the period set down in the Treaty of Versailles.

Photo: Central Press

Here are two pictures of British troops parading and marching for the last time in the Rhineland during the evacuation.

PRINCIPAL EVENTS OF 1929

JAN. 7. Death of Henry Arthur Jones, English Dramatist.

,, 10. Dr. Temple enthroned Archbishop of York.

,, 15. Kellogg Peace Pact ratified by American Senate.

FEB. 9. King moved to Craigweil House, Bognor.

,, 13. Commssr. E. J. Higgins elected General of the Salvation Army in place of General Bramwell Booth.

MAR. 11. Major H. O. D. Segrave reaches 231.36 miles per hour in his racing car at Daytona Beach.

,, 20. Death of Marshal Foch

,, 23. Cambridge won the Boat Race, 100th of the series.

APR. 12. Major Segrave knighted.

,, 14. First air mail from India arrives at Croydon.

,, 26. Record flight between England and India of 4,130 miles in 50 hours, 48 minutes by two Royal Air Force officers, Squadron-Leader A. G. Jones-Williams and Flight-Lieutenant N. H. Jenkins.

,, 27. Cup Final—Bolton Wanderers 2, Portsmouth 0.

,, 29. Centenary of the Zoological Society.

MAY 14. At Newcastle the Prince of Wales opened the North East Coast Exhibition.

,, 15. King leaves Bognor for Windsor.

,, 25. Centenary of formation of Police Force celebrated in London.

,, 30. General Election : Labour majority.

JUNE. 5. Trigo, owned by Mr. W. Barnett, won the Derby.

JUNE 7. Miss Margaret Bondfield becomes first woman Cabinet Minister.

,, 16. Death of General Bramwell Booth.

JULY 5. Pope leaves Vatican—first time for 59 years.

,, 7. King attends Thanksgiving Service at Westminster Abbey.

,, 9. Submarine H.47 in collision off Pembrokeshire : 24 lives lost.

,, 10. *Southern Cross* arrives at Croydon from Sydney, Australia, the flight having started on June 25.

,, 24. Kellogg Peace Pact signed.

,, 30. World Jamboree held at Arrowe Park near Birkenhead. 21st Anniversary of Boy Scouts Movement.

AUG. 2. Barony conferred on Sir Robert Baden-Powell.

,, 9. Duchess of Bedford's flight to India and back in 7½ days, ends at Croydon.

SEPT. 7. Great Britain wins Schneider Trophy in seaplane race over the Solent.

,, 10. A British seaplane attains a record speed of 355.8 miles an hour.

,, 20. Hatry crash : Stock Exchange sensation.

OCT. 3. Death of Dr. Stressman.

,, 11. Death of Earl of Meath, founder of Empire Day.

,, 12. R.101 biggest airship in the world makes its first voyage.

NOV. 18. Death of Mr. T. P. O'Connor, M.P., famous journalist and " Father of the House of Commons."

,, 24. Death of M. Clemenceau.

DEC. 1. Great Thames floods.

,, 12. British evacuation of Rhineland completed.

,, 23. Vice-regal train bombed near Delhi.

,, 31. Paisley cinema disaster, 70 children dead.

Photo: Topical.

YOUTH ANSWERS THE CALL OF THE OPEN AIR

365

SALVAGING THE GERMAN FLEET

Salvage work was going on in Scapa Flow to raise the sunken German Fleet which had been scuttled in 1919. On the left is the barnacle-encrusted hulk of the *Seydlitz* being towed upside down to the yards to be broken up. Notice huts for the workmen engaged in the task of salvage had been built on the under-side of the ship. Below : Men are seen working inside one of the ships which had been under water for so many years. This operation of salvaging the German Fleet was unique—nothing like it had been attempted before. Those engaged in the task often suffered severe disappointment. Once when they had raised a ship to the surface some mishap occurred before they could secure it and it sank again.

Photos: S. & G.

Following the death of Dr. Robert Bridges, O.M., on April 21, John Masefield—a seaman in early life—was appointed Poet Laureate. Above, shows the new Poet Laureate, taken at Boar's Hill, near Oxford.

Photo: Topical.

1930

*C*HE world applauded Miss Amy Johnson's solo flight to Australia in just under three weeks. She is seen here acknowledging the cheers of the welcoming crowds on her arrival at Sydney. Inset is a picture of her 'plane over Port Darwin on May 24.

Photos: S. & G.

THE new Canadian Pacific Liner, *Empress of Britain*, which was launched at Glasgow by the Prince of Wales on June 11. Here is a picture of the giant hull of the famous liner taken just after her graceful progress down the slipway into deep water. Crowds watched.

Photo: Topical.

Odhams Press Ltd.   Photo: Maycock.

Mr. George Lansbury, seen above, created London's "Lido," an open-air bathing station on the Serpentine in Hyde Park. He opened it in June. During the hot summers that followed, Lansbury's Lido was the favourite resort of thousands.

Photo : S. and G.

Photo: Topical.

Two views of the Lansbury " Lido " at the Serpentine in Hyde Park.   The innovation was welcomed enthusiastically.
It became the most popular rendezvous in London.   The public would flock there after their days work in office or factory.

THE *MISS ENGLAND II* DISASTER

Photos: Topical.

On June 13 Sir Henry Segrave, the famous motorist and sportsman, was fatally injured on Lake Windermere after having achieved a new motor-boat record in *Miss England II*. Here is a picture of the wrecked boat. Inset, Sir Henry Segrave.

In the summer of 1930, at Lords, Don Bradman, the young and famous Australian cricketer, made a great innings of 334—the highest score of the year. In the previous year in Australia, Bradman made a world's record score of 452 not out.

Photo: " Daily Herald."

The first play to be televised was Pirandello's *Man with a Flower in his Mouth,* which was performed on July 14. Mr. John L. Baird, a pioneer, who for many years had experimented with television, is seen here watching the performance.

FIRST AIR MAIL PILLAR BOX

THE tremendous development of aviation during the war greatly assisted the organisation of regular air-mail traffic between important centres. In particular, the business community found the service a great boon and increasing use was made of it. In July the first of the blue air-mail pillar boxes was erected in the Strand.

KING'S PRIZE WON BY WOMAN

THE King's Prize at Bisley was this year won for the first time by a woman, Miss M.E.Foster, who, in the picture below, is seen at the range.

Photos: Topical and S. and G.

Inset Photo: S. and G.

On October 5 the world was shocked by the wreck of the R101 during a storm at Beauvais in France.   The airship struck a hillside, exploded, and burst into flames.   Only six out of a total of fifty-four crew and passengers were saved, among the dead being Lord Thomson (Secretary of State for Air) and Sir Sefton Brancker (Director of Civil Aviation).

The picture shows the burnt-out skeleton of the airship lying partially across field and forest.   It gives a vivid indication of the airship's enormous size.   Inset : The scale model of the airship that was used during the inquiry, into the disaster conducted by Sir John Simon and two assessors, which resulted in the abandonment of all airship construction by Great Britain.

The Pari-Mutuel System of wagering, successfully conducted in France and other countries, came into general use in England during this year. Inset, is an electric Totalisator machine in use at a race meeting during the summer.

EARL OF
BALFOUR

EARL OF
BIRKENHEAD

DEATH OF TWO
FAMOUS STATESMEN

THIS year witnessed the death of two famous British statesmen.   The Earl of Balfour (above), who died on March
19 after a brilliant political career.   He first became a
Member of Parliament in 1874, representing the Conservative
interests at Hertford.   Among the important public offices
he held were those of Chief Secretary for Ireland, First
Lord of the Treasury and Leader of the House of Commons in 1891, Prime Minister in 1902, First Lord of the
Admiralty in 1915, Foreign Secretary in 1916 and Lord
President of the Council in Mr. Baldwin's second Ministry.

ON September 30 the Earl of Birkenhead died.   As "F.E.,"
he leapt into prominence as a brilliant politician and
lawyer.   He became Solicitor-General, and also Attorney-
General in 1915 in which year he was knighted.   In 1918
he accepted the Lord Chancellorship and was raised to the
peerage in 1919.   In 1924 he became Secretary of State for
India resigning in 1928 to take up a commercial career.

PRINCIPAL EVENTS OF 1930

JAN. 3. Prince of Wales left England for tour in South Africa.

,, 16. Airship R100 in a trial flight, reaches 81½ miles an hour.

,, 21. Five Power Naval Conference opened by His Majesty.

,, 22. Death of Viscount Esher.

FEB. 17. Death of Madame Kirkby Lunn, Mezzo-Soprano.
Mr. MacDonald resigns membership of I.L.P.

,, 26. Death of Cardinal Raffaele Merry del Val, Pontifical Secretary of State.

MAR. 2. Death of D. H. Lawrence, novelist.

,, 6. Death of Viscount Gladstone.
Death of Grand-Admiral Alfred von Tirpitz, of the German Navy.

,, 19. Death of Earl of Balfour.

APR. 4. Death of Queen of Sweden.

,, 12. Cambridge win the Boat Race; 41 wins to Oxford's 40.

,, 16. Trade agreement reached between U.S.S.R. and Great Britain.

,, 21. Death of Robert Bridges, Poet Laureate.

,, 26. Graf Zeppelin visits England and cruises over London.

,, 30. Wireless telephony opened between England and Australia.
Duchess of Bedford flies back from Cape in 19½ days.

MAY 5. Amy Johnson starts flight to Australia.

,, 9. John Masefield appointed Poet Laureate, succeeding late Robert Bridges.

,, 10. Amy Johnson reaches Karachi.

,, 13. Death of Dr. Nansen, Arctic Explorer and Scientist.

., 15. Death of William J. Locke, novelist.

,, 24. Amy Johnson arrives at Port Darwin.

,, 25. Death of Randall Davidson, Archbishop of Canterbury.

JUNE 4. Aga Khan's colt Blenheim wins Derby.

,, 11. New liner, *Empress of Britain*, launched at Glasgow by Prince of Wales.

,, 13. Sir Henry Segrave fatally injured on Lake Windermere.

JUNE 25. Kingsford Smith flight from Ireland to Newfoundland.

,, 28. White Star motor liner *Britannic*, largest British motor vessel, sailed from Liverpool to New York on her maiden voyage.

,, 30. Occupation by foreign troops of German territory ends after eleven years.

JULY 7. Death of Sir Arthur Conan Doyle.

,, 19. Miss Foster (first woman winner) wins King's prize at Bisley.

,, 23. Violent earthquakes near Naples.

AUG. 1. R100 arrives in Montreal from Cardington in 79 hours.

,, 16. R100 reaches Cardington from Montreal in 57 hours.

,, 19. Sydney Harbour Bridge joined.

,, 21. Birth of a second daughter to Duke and Duchess of York (Princess Margaret Rose).

SEPT. 3. Capt. Costes and Lieut. Bellonte arrive in New York after having flown from Paris in 37 hours, 18 minutes.

,, 10. Miss Peggy Duncan, swims Channel in 16 hours, 7 minutes.

,, 15. Centenary celebrations of opening of Liverpool-Manchester Railway.

,, 29. Death of William Pett Ridge, author.

,, 30. Death of Earl of Birkenhead (F. E. Smith)

OCT. 1. Wei-Hai-Wei given back to China.

,, 5. Disaster to R101 at Beauvais; 48 out of 54 lost their lives including Lord Thomson and Sir Sefton Brancker.

,, 19. Wing Commander Kingsford Smith flies from England to Port Darwin in just under 10 days.

,, 26. Coal mine disaster in the Saar.

NOV. 2. Emperor of Abyssinia crowned.

,, 12. India Round Table Conference in London.

,, 14. Imperial Conference concluded.

,, 25. Earthquake in Japan.

DEC. 19. Lord Willingdon appointed Viceroy of India.

,, 27. Death of Lord Melchett.

FLIGHT FROM THE £

Photos : S. and G. and Topical

During 1931, Britain held a number of speed records. Malcolm Campbell broke the world's motor speed record when on February 5, he reached a speed of 246.154 miles per hour in his racing car, *Bluebird*, on Daytona Beach. He was knighted on his return to England. The picture shows the *Bluebird* in action. Inset : Sir Malcolm Campbell.

Photo : Topical

On July 9, Kaye Don (inset) broke the water speed record on Lake Garda, with a speed of 110 miles per hour. In the same year, at Detroit, Commodore Gar Wood, piloting *Miss America IX*, beat Kaye Don in the Harmsworth Trophy contest. This picture shows the race between the British and American boats in progress. Note the terrific spray.

Photos : S and G. and Flight

Great Britain captured the air speed record when, on September 13, Lieutenant Boothman won the Schneider Trophy outright. Lieutenant Boothman and two other pilots are seen above, going out to their 'plane, and, below, lined up at their base at Calshot. The world 3-kilometre speed record was broken on the same day by Lieutenant Stainforth.

Photo : *Topical*

The railways also added to the number of records held by Britain this year. *The Cheltenham Flyer* established a record for the world's fastest train by reaching a speed of 78 m.p.h., while the next year the L.N.E.R. established a new record when the *Flying Scotsman* made the non-stop journey of 392¼ miles from London to Edinburgh in 7 hours 27 minutes.

Photos : S. and G.

Photo : Topical

ENGLAND
TO
AUSTRALIA—
MORE
RECORDS

A FURTHER air record was set up by C. W. A. Scott (right), who flew from England to Australia, arriving on April 10—in 9 days, 3 hours, 40 mins. Jim Mollison flew from Australia to England in 8 days, 20 hours, 19 mins. and arrived on August 6. The picture above shows Mollison's 'plane arriving at Croydon. Inset : Mr. Mollison.

The bank rate falls. Clerks rushing out of the Bank to let the brokers on the Stock Exchange hear the news.

Photo : Topical

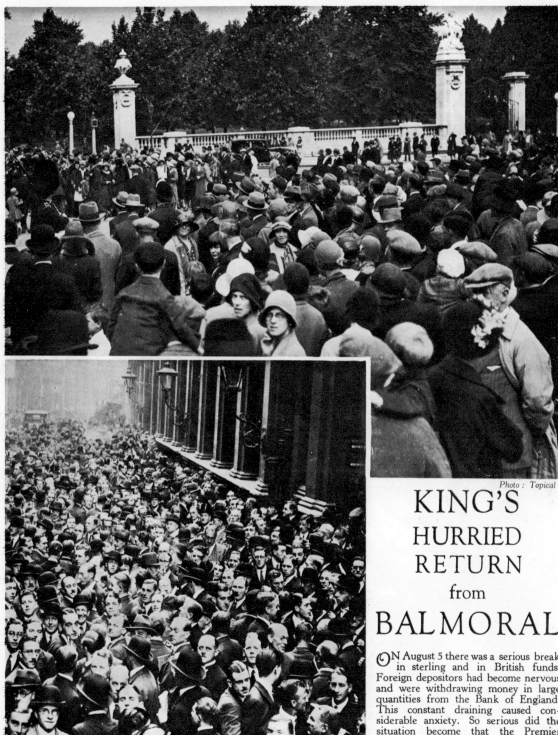

Photo : Topical

KING'S
HURRIED
RETURN
from
BALMORAL

ON August 5 there was a serious break in sterling and in British funds. Foreign depositors had become nervous and were withdrawing money in large quantities from the Bank of England. This constant draining caused considerable anxiety. So serious did the situation become that the Premier returned to London on August 11, and the King from Balmoral a few days later. Above : The crowd outside Buckingham Palace awaiting the King's return, and (left) the seething crowd outside the Stock Exchange during the crisis.

On August 24 the Labour Government resigned and a new administration, headed by Mr. Ramsay Macdonald, took office. The new Cabinet (seen here) consisted of ten members only : Front row, reading from left to right : Lord Snowden, Mr. Ramsay Macdonald and Mr. Stanley Baldwin. Second row : Sir P. Cunliffe-Lister, Mr. J. H. Thomas, and Lord Reading. Third row : Sir Herbert Samuel and Lord Sankey. Fourth row : Mr. Neville Chamberlain and Sir Samuel Hoare. On September 20 a fresh crisis arose. A General Election took place in October and a " National Government " with an economy policy was returned by a large majority.

" Daily Herald " Photos : Jarché

During September, in connection with the International Illumination Congress, London buildings were floodlit and a new city was revealed to delighted spectators. Above is the Shell-Mex Building and Victoria Embankment as they appeared and, below, Buckingham Palace. Well-known buildings in many other cities and towns were also illuminated.

Photo : Topical

In October of this year a mass demonstration of an entirely peaceful nature, by Civil Servants, took place in London against the salary cuts necessitated by the severely economical policy imposed as a result of the general financial situation.

Another controversy of great public interest during this year was the Sunday Cinema's Bill. After much discussion, the Bill was dropped and a temporary measure was passed legalising the existing practice. An Act regularising the whole position was passed in 1932. Above is a Sunday cinema queue, indicating the popularity of this form of entertainment.

" Daily Herald " Photo : Jarche

The Government decided to go off the Gold Standard. Foreign traders hastened to complete their orders before the change in the value of the pound. The Pool of London, seen above, was for many weeks a scene of feverish activity.

Photo : S. and G.

On December 11 it was announced that owing to the prevailing depression and the need for economy, work on the Cunarder " 534 " would have to be suspended. This picture shows the work-people leaving the yards on the last day.

" Daily Herald " Photo : Jarché

A sombre picture of the half-finished hull of the Cunard liner " 534." Over two years later—in 1934—work on this liner was resumed. The " 534 " when launched by the Queen on September 26, 1934, was christened *Queen Mary*.

PRINCIPAL EVENTS OF 1931

JAN. 3. Death of Marshal Joseph Jacques Césaire Joffre, French soldier.

,, 4. Death of the Princess Royal—Princess Louise, the King's eldest sister.

,, 16. The Prince of Wales accompanied by Prince George left London for Paris by air on the first stage of their tour to South Africa.

,, 19. India Round Table Conference ends.

,, 22. Death of Anna Pavlova.

,, 29. In an explosion at the Whitehaven Colliery, 26 men lost their lives.

FEB. 3. Earthquake in New Zealand. Town of Napier destroyed.

,, 4. Lady Houston's guarantee of £100,000 for Schneider Trophy.

,, 5. Malcolm Campbell breaks world's motor speed record at 246 m.p.h. at Daytona.

,, 10. Viceroy Lord Irwin inaugurates New Delhi as capital of India.

,, 19. Mrs. Victor Bruce arrives at Lympne after world flight.

,, 21. Malcolm Campbell knighted.

,, 23. Death of Dame Nellie Melba.

,, 28. Sir Oswald Mosley forms new party.

MAR. 21. Cambridge won the Boat Race, their 8th successive victory.

,, 22. " Royal Scot " train wrecked near Leighton Buzzard; 6 deaths.

,, 26. Death of Timothy Michael Healy, first Governor-General of the Irish Free State.

,, 27. Death of Arnold Bennett; novelist and dramatist.

APR. 2. Kay Don breaks world's motor boat speed record, reaching 103.49 miles an hour.

,, 4. First official air mail for Australia leaves Croydon.

,, 6. Glen Kidston reaches Capetown after record flight of 6½ days.

,, 10. C. W. A. Scott creates record by flying to Australia in 9 days, 4 hours, 11 minutes.

,, 14. Abdication of King Alphonso of Spain.

,, 26. Census taken.

MAY 14. First air mail from Australia.

,, 22. Whipsnade Zoo opened.

,, 27. Professor Piccard ascends nearly 10 miles in balloon.

JUNE 3. Derby won by Mr. J. A. Dewar's Cameronian.

,, 5. C. W. A. Scott makes record flight from Australia to Lympne (10 days, 13 hours).

,, 9. British submarine, *Poseidon*, sunk off Wei-hai-Wei; 20 lives lost.

JULY 10. King opens George V dock at Glasgow.

,, 27. Death of Viscount Knutsford.

AUG. 6. J. A. Mollison beats C. W. A. Scott's record in flight from Australia to England. Time 8 days 22 hrs. 25 min.

,, 18. Graf Zeppelin flew from Friedrichshafen to London and toured over England.

,, 23. Labour Government resigns.

,, 24. Mr. Ramsay MacDonald forms National Government.

,, 31. Death of Sir Thomas Henry Hall Caine; novelist.

SEPT. 13. Britain finally wins Schneider Trophy; third consecutive victory.

,, 14. " Cheltenham Flyer" establishes record for world's fastest train, 78 m.p.h.

,, 21. Britain off Gold Standard.

,, 29. Fl.-Lt. G. H. Stainforth makes world air speed record 408.8 m.p.h.

,, 29. Death of Sir William Orpen; British artist.

OCT. 2. Death of Sir Thomas Lipton, merchant and yachtsman.

,, 8. Lord Trenchard appointed Commissioner of the Police of the Metropolis in succession to Viscount Byng, who resigned.

,, 18. Death of Thomas Alva Edison, world-famous inventor.

,, 27. General Election: Majority for National Government.

NOV. 5. Miss Peggy Salaman and Mr. Gordon Stone complete new record flight to the Cape (5 days, 6 hours, 40 minutes).

,, 9. A. C. Butler sets up new record in flight from England to Port Darwin (9 days, 2 hours, 29 minutes).

DEC. 10. Nobel Peace Prize for 1931 divided between Miss Jane Addams and Dr. Nicholas Murray Butler.

., 30. Mr. Fielder, a British air pilot, flew from London to Algiers in a day.

THE CHILDREN'S CHARTER
Children and Young Persons Act—July

On January 24 a mutiny broke out in Dartmoor Prison in the course of which warders and hastily summoned troops were assisted by some of the convicts themselves in quelling the disturbance. After an inquiry had been held, a report was issued and the mutineers stood their trial. Twenty-one convicts were sentenced to further terms of penal servitude. The pictures show, above, an aerial view of the prison and, below, the buildings set on fire by the mutineers.

DEATH OF EDGAR WALLACE

*W*HILE on a visit to America, Edgar Wallace, then the most popular writer of crime fiction in the world, was taken seriously ill and died on February 10. *Left:* A characteristic picture of Edgar Wallace at the wheel of his boat with his familiar cigarette holder.

*I*N February the much discussed Tariff Duties came before Parliament, and the Bill was passed. So, early in the year, Britain, after eighty years, formally abandoned her Free Trade policy. Although some measures had been taken the year before against dumping, the Tariff Bill caused tremendous activity at the docks, and the picture below shows a ship unloading goods in a last-minute endeavour to get them into Britain before import duties came into force.

Photo: Topical

Mr. Lang, the Premier of New South Wales, opened Sydney Harbour Bridge, seen above, on March 19.   This colossal
engineering feat cost nearly £10,000,000 and, as is indicated by the picture, saves a journey of many miles round the harbour.
The bridge, which is the largest single span in the world, is entirely of British workmanship and materials.

Photos : Topical

In the early months of 1932 many people took advantage of the increased value of gold. Jewellers' shops displayed such notices as "We Give the Highest Price for Gold," and large numbers disposed of old jewellery and hoarded sovereigns. In the picture above is a view of gold being weighed before purchase. Below, a crowd attracted by a jeweller's offer.

APRIL 23 marked the opening of the
new Shakespeare Memorial Theatre
at Stratford-on-Avon by the Prince of
Wales. The winning design for the
splendid building to take the place of the
theatre destroyed by fire, was submitted
by a woman, Miss Elizabeth Scott.

Photo : " Times "

Photo : S. and G.

It is not generally realised that the street lighting of Piccadilly was not electrified until May 9 of this year. The picture shows London's famous centre—known as "the hub of the universe"—on its brilliant "first night." Eros, which had been removed during the reconstruction of the Underground Station, can be seen replaced in its original position.

Photo: Central Press.

On May 14 the broadcasting station at Savoy Hill, known as 2LO, gave its last programme before removing to its magnificent new home—Broadcasting House—seen on the page on the right. *Above :* The aerial masts of 2LO—a familar sight to Londoners.

Photos : B.B.C.

Broadcasting House, Portland Place, London—the headquarters of the British Broadcasting Corporation. *Inset :* The announcer saying the familiar " Good night, everybody—Good night " for the last time before leaving Savoy Hill.

The Lausanne Conference opened on June 16 to discuss the question of Reparations. It was hoped that there would be

EUCHARISTIC CONGRESS

A magnificent scene during the great Eucharistic Congress held in Dublin in June to which Catholics from all over the world

a definite cancellation of War Debts, but the agreement that was ultimately signed on July 9 fell short of this ideal.

AT DUBLIN   *Photos : S. and G.*

had flocked. This picture shows the altar erected on a bridge over the Liffey at which a service is being conducted.

Photo : S. and G.

London's newest bridge, which links Millbank with Lambeth, was opened by the King on July 19.   The picture shows
the crowds that thronged the bridge immediately after the ceremony.   Lambeth Palace can be seen in the background.

Photo : S. and G.

Representatives of Great Britain and the Dominions gathered at Ottawa on July 22 to discuss Imperial Preference and Tariffs. The above photograph shows a general view of the Assembly inside the Canadian Government Buildings.

Odhams Press Ltd.   Photo : Maycock

TWO
LITERARY
EVENTS

*T*HE Nobel Prize for Literature was awarded to John Galsworthy, O.M. (*right*), on November 10. This famous novelist and playwright is chiefly remembered for his novels collected under the title of " The Forsyte Saga." Mr. Galsworthy fell seriously ill early in 1933 and died on January 31 of that year.

(*Circle*) J. B. Priestley, who had already come into popular favour with his " Good Companions," produced his first play, *Dangerous Corner*, which was one of the most successful plays of the year.

Photo : S. and G.

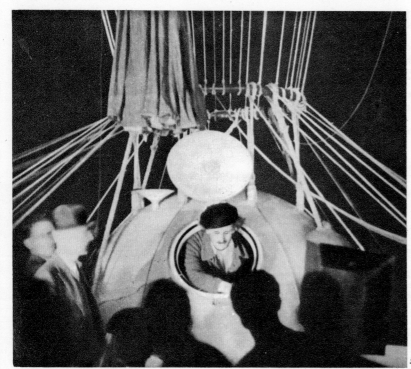

EXPLORING THE STRATOSPHERE

PROFESSOR PICCARD —the Belgian scientist —on August 17 ascended to a height of 16,700 metres in his second attempt to explore the stratosphere. His discoveries may lead to tremendous developments of aerial transport at high altitudes.

Photo : S. and G

On December 15, £20,000,000 in the vaults of the Bank of England was transferred to America, and later, actual gold to this value was shipped across to the United States. Our picture shows a part of one such shipment leaving London. It was feared that after the financial stringency of the last months such a drain on our gold supplies would affect the pound. But the act of paying reflected so well on the credit of the country that the pound actually increased in value.

PRINCIPAL EVENTS OF 1932

JAN. 1. Princess Mary created Princess Royal.

,, 19. Kingsford-Smith lands at Port Darwin with air mail from England.

,, 20. First regular air mail service opened between London and Cape Town.

,, 24. Mutiny at Dartmoor Prison; 80 convicts injured.

,, 26. British submarine M2 lost with the whole crew.

FEB. 2. Rt. Hon. Arthur Henderson opens Disarmament Conference at Geneva.

,, 10. Death of Edgar Wallace, English journalist.

,, 11. Publication of Import Duties Bill, imposing 10 per cent duty on almost all imported goods.

,, 24. At Daytona Beach, Florida, Sir Malcolm Campbell made a new record of 253.968 m.p.h.

,, 29. Tariff Bill comes into force. England a protectionist country after 80 years of Free Trade.

MAR. 5. Death of John Philip Sousa, American conductor and composer.

,, 7. Death of Aristide Briand, eleven times Premier of France.

,, 9. Mr. de Valera elected President of Irish Free State.

,, 19. Sydney Harbour Bridge officially opened.
Cambridge wins Boat Race.

,, 28. Mr. J. A. Mollison reaches Capetown after a flight from England of 4 days, 17 hours, 19 minutes, beating the record by 15 hours, 18 minutes.

APR. 23. Cup Tie Final at Wembley; Newcastle United 2, Arsenal 1.

,, 23. New Shakespeare Memorial Theatre, Stratford-on-Avon, opened by Prince of Wales.

,, 27. Mr. C. W. A. Scott flew from Lympne to Darwin, N. Australia, in 8 days, 20 hours, 47 minutes.

MAY 6. Assassination of Paul Doumer, President of the French Republic.

,, 10. M. Lebrun elected President of France.

,, 14. Last programme broadcast from Savoy Hill.

,, 22. Miss Amelia Earhart first woman to fly Atlantic.

,, 23. Death of Earl of Inchcape.

JUNE 1. April the Fifth, owned by Tom Walls, wins the Derby.

JUNE 6. Great Western Railway express breaks record for speed by travelling from Swindon to Paddington, average speed 81.6 m.p.h.

,, 15. Death of Sir Donald Maclean, M.P.

,, 16. Mr. MacDonald opens Lausanne Conference on reparations and war debts.

JULY 1. Mr. de Valera refuses to pay British Government £1,500,000 due on account of land annuities.

,, 2. Death of Dom Manoel, ex-King of Portugal.

,, 16. Death of Field-Marshal Viscount Plumer.

,, 18. Kaye Don reaches 119.81 m.p.h. on Loch Lomond.

,, 19. King and Queen open new Lambeth Bridge.

AUG. 17. Professor Piccard ascends nearly $10\frac{1}{2}$ miles in balloon.

,, 19. Mr. J. A. Mollison makes Transatlantic flight from Ireland to New Brunswick in $30\frac{1}{4}$ hours.

SEPT. 12. "World's Fastest Train," the Cheltenham Flyer, completed the journey between Swindon and Paddington (G.W.R.) in 65 minutes, an average speed of 71.3 m.p.h.

,, 16. Death of Sir Ronald Ross, pioneer of conquest of malaria.

,, 28. Lord Snowden, Sir Arthur Sinclair and Sir Herbert Samuel resign on Tariffs.

OCT. 3. Annual Conference of Labour Party at Leicester.

,, 18. Rt. Hon. Arthur Henderson resigns leadership of Labour Party.

,, 25. Mr. G. Lansbury becomes Chairman and Leader of the Parliamentary Labour Party.

,, 30. Death of Field-Marshal Lord Methuen.

NOV. 10. Mr. Franklin Roosevelt elected President of U.S.A.

,, 18. Mrs. Mollison successfully landed at Cape having taken 4 days, 6 hours, 54 minutes on her journey from England.

DEC. 6. Death of Eugene Brieux, French dramatist.

,, 19. Mrs. Mollison completes homeward flight from the Cape in 7 days, 7 hours, 5 minutes, having beaten record for return journey.

Photo : " Times "

This photograph, which shows the famous Underwriters' Room at Lloyd's, is of especial interest in connection with the disaster of the *Atlantique*—Lloyd's was involved with the insurance to an extent of nearly £1,000,000.

Photo : Topical

On January 4 the huge French liner *Atlantique* caught fire and drifted in flames for some days before it grounded. Above is an aerial view of the burning vessel. At the enquiry faulty electric wiring was put forward as a cause of the fire.

Photo : Central Press

The World Economic Conference, which was attended by representatives of all the great powers, was opened in the
Geological Museum at South Kensington by the King on June 12. It failed to combat the almost world-wide depression.

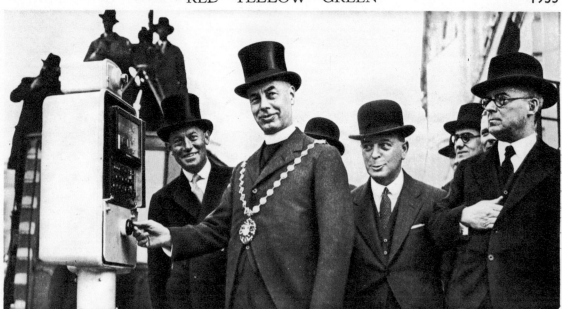

Photo : S. and G.

Progress in automatic traffic control—the Mayor of Westminster inaugurates the new system in Trafalgar Square

Photo : Topical

Great Britain won the Davis Cup for the first time in twenty-two years, when the British team played in Paris on July 30.
Above, left to right : H. G. N. Lee, F. J. Perry, H. Roper Barrett (non-playing captain), H. W. Austin, G. P. Hughes.

Photos : S. and G.

LADY HOUSTON financed an expedition, with Air-Commodore Fellowes as Technical Adviser, to attempt to fly over Everest. On April 3 two machines of the expedition, piloted by the Marquess of Douglas and Clydesdale and Flight-Lieutenant McIntyre, cleared the summit, which up to this time had never been conquered despite the repeated attempts of mountaineers. The flight was completed in exactly three hours Here is a magnificent view of Mount Everest, the highest mountain in the world, and (inset) one of the planes that at last conquered the heights that claimed so many lives.

Photo : By permission of the Royal Geographical Society

Photo : Topical

On February 6 a mass Labour Demonstration against the Government's economy measures, cuts in salaries and unemployment benefit, was held in Hyde Park, and was addressed by Mr. George Lansbury (seen above), and by other Labour leaders.

Photo : " Times "

A charming study of the two little daughters of the Duke and Duchess of York, Princess Elizabeth and Princess Margaret Rose. The picture was taken in the " grounds " of the model house presented to Princess Elizabeth by the people of Wales.

Photos : L.P.T.B.

On July 1 the newly formed London Passenger Transport Board took over the London buses, underground railways, trams and motor-coaches. Considerable progress has been made under the Board. These two pictures show the latest developments of the tube system. (*Above*) the booking hall of Manor House Station (*below*) one of the latest trains.

Public interest was focused on Russia when it was learned that six British subjects had been arrested in Moscow on certain serious charges. Two of the party, Messrs. Thornton and MacDonald, were sentenced to imprisonment, but were afterwards released as a result of diplomatic negotiations. They are seen above on their arrival back in England.

FROM
SLUMS
TO
SUNSHINE

*T*HE problem of the slums—with their terrible overcrowding and sunless homes—is one of the greatest facing the country to-day. To clear the slums and to replace them with cheerful houses is to make a real contribution to the health and happiness of the people. This badly needed reform is at last being given serious attention.

Photos : " Weekly Illustrated "

The Government launched this year a campaign with the object of demolishing slum property all over the country and re-housing the population within a period of five years.   The cost of the whole scheme was estimated at £115,000,000, with employment provided for many more workers during the five years.   The pictures on the left-hand page draws comparison between the conditions as they exist in some parts to-day and (above) the ideal to which Britain's "Five-Year Plan" is striving.   Sir E. Hilton Young is the Minister responsible for these plans, but before him Mr. Arthur Greenwood, M.P., the former Minister, laid the foundations.

Photo : " Weekly Illustrated "

Photo : " Times "

On July 19 the huge Masonic Temple in Great Queen Street, London, was opened by the Duke of Connaught, Grand Master of the United Grand Lodge of England. This memorial, dedicated to Peace, was paid for by voluntary subscriptions.

Photo : " Times "

The largest dry dock in the world was opened with great ceremony at Southampton by the King and the Queen on July 26 and the Queen christened it with Empire wine " the King George V Graving Dock."

THE THAMES EMBANK-MENT TO-DAY, LOOKING FROM THE SOUTH SIDE.

Photo : " Times "

Photos : S. and G.

The anti-Jewish campaign in Germany aroused widespread protest. Great Britain became a refuge for many German subjects who had been driven from their own country. *Above* : Is a typical example of anti-Jewish propaganda in Berlin and (*below*) the end of a protest meeting in a London cinema—typical of many which were held during the summer.

By permission of the Manchester Art Gallery

"Cock o' the North," by Keith Henderson, one of the pictures that attracted great attention in this year's Royal Academy.

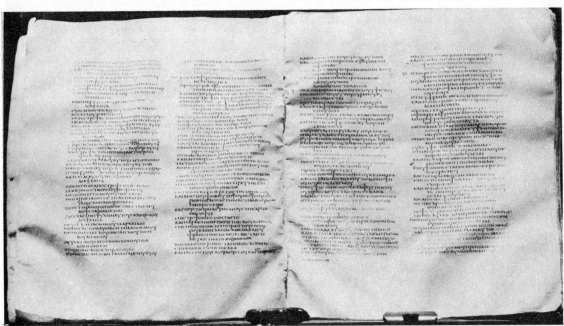

"Daily Herald" Photo Jarché

At the end of the year the government agreed to pay part of the purchase price of the famous *Codex Sinaiticus*, one of the earliest known Greek manuscripts of the Bible, which was accordingly purchased from Russia for £100,000. A public subscription was opened to raise the balance of the purchase price. The Codex is now in the British Museum.

PRINCIPAL EVENTS OF 1933

JAN. 3. National Playing Fields Association granted a Royal Charter.

,, 31. Death of John Galsworthy, novelist and playwright.

FEB. 8. Squadron-Leader O. R. Gayford and Flight-Lieut. G. E. Nicholetts establish a non-stop record of 5,309 miles.

,, 9. J. A. Mollison made record flight to Brazil.

,, 12. Death of Field-Marshal Sir William Robertson.

,, 22. Sir Malcolm Campbell sets up new motor speed record, 272.108 miles an hour.

MAR. 9. Ramsay MacDonald and Sir John Simon leave for Geneva to attend the Disarmament Conference.

,, 19. Death of E. Temple Thurston, novelist and dramatist.

,, 28. The Imperial Airways Liner, *City of Liverpool* on the London-Brussels-Cologne service, caught fire near Dixmude. 15 lives lost.

APR. 1. Cambridge won the Boat Race.

,, 2. Death of The Maharajah of Nawanagar (Ranjitsinghi).

,, 3. Aeroplanes fly over peak of Mount Everest.

,, 4. The U.S. naval airship *Akron*, carrying 77 officers and men, crashed into the sea on the New Jersey coast, 74 lives lost.

,, 10. Warrant Officer Agello, of the Italian Air Force, beat the world's record (hitherto held by Great Britain) by attaining an average speed of 423 miles an hour.

,, 15. Prime Minister leaves for Washington to discuss plans for World Economic Conference.

,, 26. Mr. Justice McCardie found shot dead.

,, 27. Death of Sir Geoffrey Salmond, Air Chief Marshal.

MAY 3. Oath of Allegiance removed from Irish Free State Constitution.

,, 24. Death of Admiral of the Fleet, Lord Wester Wemyss.

,, 31. Lord Derby's " Hyperion " won the Derby.

JUN. 12. King opens the World Economic Conference at the Geological Museum, South Kensington.

JUN. 15. Britain pays 10,000,000 dollars in silver to the United States of America.

JULY 1. London Passenger Transport Board commenced control.

,, 14. Death of Concemore Thomas Cramp, General Secretary of the National Union of Railwaymen.

,, 19. Mr. Angus Miller crossed the Channel between Dover and Calais and back in the record time of 1 hour, 45 seconds, in his motor boat, *White Cloud II.*

,, 20. Death of Viscount Burnham, newspaper proprietor.

,, 23. Mr. and Mrs. Mollison, who left Carmarthenshire at noon on July 22 on a flight to New York, succeeded in crossing the Atlantic, but crashed at Bridgeport, Long Island Sound.

,, 26. King opens world's biggest dry dock at Southampton.

,, 27. Conclusion of World Economic Conference.

,, 30. Great Britain, after twenty years, again won the Davis Cup for lawn tennis.

AUG. 23. King and Queen opened the new Civic Hall at Leeds.

SEPT. 7. Death of Viscount Grey of Fallodon.

,, 20. Death of Mrs. Annie Besant, social reformer and leading Theosophist. Lived in India for many years.

OCT. 14. Germany leaves the Disarmament Conference and later resigned from the League of Nations.

,, 19. Charles Ulm and his companions landed in Western Australia after flying from England in 6 days, 17 hours, 56 minutes.

DEC. 5. Prohibition ended in U.S.A.

,, 23. The worst disaster in the history of the French Railways occurred near Lagny, 15 miles from Paris, over 200 people were killed in a collision.

,, 24. The *Codex Sinaiticus*, purchased from the Soviet Government for £100,000 arrived in London and was placed in the British Museum.

,, 30. Ten killed in Imperial Airways Liner crash at Ruysselede.

BELISHA BEACONS

LONDON'S LABOUR GOVERNMENT

*I*N March, the Labour Party secured a large majority in the London County Council Elections. This was the first time Labour had been in power in the County Hall. On the left is Lord Snell, chairman of the County Council, and below, Mr. Herbert Morrison, the leader of the Labour Party in the Council. Immediately after election, a number of progressive measures were put in hand by the new administration.

Photos : Odhams Press Ltd. Maycock

Among the greatest steps made in social progress is the careful safeguarding of the health of children. These two pictures of a dental clinic run in conjunction with the schools, show how children are cared for in many of the elementary schools to-day. *Above :* The nurse comes to fetch the next patient for the dentist and none of the children looks in the least frightened at the idea of what is before them. *Below :* The examination in progress while the mother stands by.

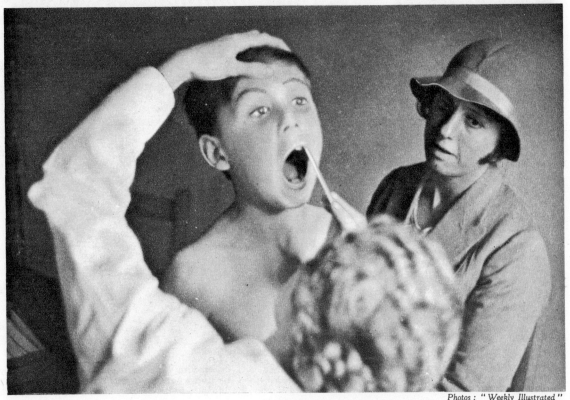

Photos : " Weekly Illustrated "

Photo : Topical

After ten years of discussion it was finally decided by the new L.C.C. to demolish Waterloo Bridge and erect an entirely new structure. Subsidence of the foundations occurred in 1924 and the bridge was temporarily repaired. On June 20, 1934, demolition operations, seen here in progress, began and the bridge was finally closed to traffic on the 22nd.

THE YEAR
of the
GREAT DROUGHT

BRITAIN is a country famous for its copious rainfall, but for the second year in succession, the summer of 1934 was one of extreme drought, and on June 27, restrictions were imposed on the use of water in London. Country districts suffered severely and scenes like that on the right, where villagers are buying pails of water, were quite common. *Above*: A modern version of Jack and Jill.

GREAT BRITAIN'S SINGLES DOUBLE!

GREAT BRITAIN scored two remarkable successes at Wimbledon
this year when Miss Dorothy Round
(*right*) won the women's championship
by defeating Miss Helen Jacobs of
America; and F. J. Perry conquered
J. Crawford, Australia, in final of the
men's singles. To carry off dual honours
in the same season was truly a fine
achievement for Great Britain after
many years when no victory in either
of these classic events had been scored.

Photos : " Weekly Illustrated "

A remarkable photograph of four of Britain's crack jockeys. Reading from left to right : Steve Donoghue, Joe Childs, Fred Fox, and Brownie Carslake. Donoghue and Childs celebrated their fiftieth birthday in 1934.

Photo : Odhams Press Ltd. Jarché.

MIRACLE
OF THE
MERSEY

ON July 18 H.M. the King opened the Mersey Tunnel at Liverpool—the construction of which was one of the greatest engineering feats of the century. These two pictures give a graphic idea of the task of the workmen, who were working all the time under the bed of the River Mersey. On the right-hand page is the opening ceremony taking place. The King's car is seen just entering the finished tunnel.

Photos : " Weekly Illustrated "

During this year two dramatic revolts occurred in Austria. In February, there was a Socialist rising and troops were called out. The top picture shows a wrecked room in the Karl Marx building—a block of Municipal flats which were heavily shelled by the troops, many people being killed and wounded before the revolt was quelled and order restored.

Trouble broke out again in July when disguised Nazis attempted a *coup d'etat*. The wireless station was seized. Dr. Dollfuss, the chancellor, was taken prisoner and afterwards assassinated in circumstances of great inhumanity. Government troops later regained control of the situation. The picture shows the wireless station being stormed by government soldiers.

Armed troops in the streets of Vienna, after the assassination of Dr. Dollfuss. (*Inset*) Dr. Dollfuss lying in state.

Photo : *Odhams Press Ltd. Jarche*

THE COMING
of
CHEAP
ELECTRICITY

THE grid system which will eventually bring cheap electricity to every country village, had its only serious breakdown on July 29. Thirteen counties were affected. Sunday dinners were spoilt, and electric trains stopped running. The above picture shows Battersea Power station which supplies most of London and Greater London, and (*on right*) Barking Power station's greatest pylon which is the highest in Great Britain.

Photo : *" Daily Herald "*

On September 26, the Queen launched the Cunard-White Star liner, 534, and christened it *Queen Mary*.

Photo : Topical

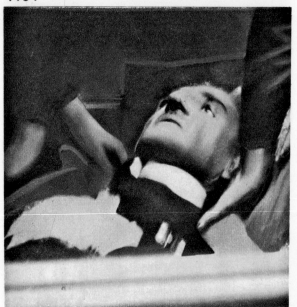

ASSASSINATION OF A KING

ON October 9 the whole world was shocked by the assassination of King Alexander of Yugoslavia, and M. Barthou, French Minister for Foreign Affairs. King Alexander had just landed at Marseilles on a state visit to France, and had been met by M. Barthou. During the drive through the streets of Marseilles in an open car, the assassin sprang on the running board of the car and fired point blank at the two men. The photograph shows (*left*) King Alexander as he fell back into the car, (*below*) the panic the moment realisation dawned on the onlookers, and (*inset*) the assassin, so roughly handled by the crowd that he died of his injuries.

Photo: Topical

THE greatest air race of the century started from Mildenhall at 6.30 a.m. on October 20, when aeroplanes of all countries competed in the England-Australia flight. The prize offered was £10,000 and a £500 gold cup. The contest was won for Great Britain by Mr. T. Campbell Black and Mr. C. W. A. Scott in a De Havilland Comet. They completed the flight in the marvellous time of 2 days, 22 hours and 58 minutes.

Photo : Topical

TO
AUSTRALIA
IN UNDER
3 DAYS !

THE top photograph shows Mr. C. W. A. Scott being cheered on his arrival in Australia. *On the left :* The commentator broadcasts the start of the race from Mildenhall, and *(below)* a picture taken at dawn of the line up of some of the competitors' 'planes.

Photo : Marconi

Photo : Topical

In December British troops were sent out to the Saar as part of an international police force to keep order during the taking of the plebiscite. The people of the Saar were to vote as to whether they wished to belong to Germany, to France, or to become a self-governing community under the League of Nations. The picture shows the landing of the troops.

Photo : Odhams Press Ltd. Maycock

The Minister of Agriculture, faced with a surplus production of milk, put forward a scheme early in 1934 for the supply of milk at a special rate to school children. Not until the end of the year did the scheme come into operation : by it some millions of children were drinking nearly half a pint of milk daily. It was supplied to them at the price of a halfpenny.

The scene in Westminster Abbey on November 29, when H.R.H. the Duke of Kent was married to Princess Marina.

ROMANCE
of the KING'S
YOUNGEST
SON

ON August 28, the betrothal of Prince George, youngest son of the King, to Princess Marina of Greece was announced. In October the King conferred on his son the title of the Duke of Kent. The marriage took place on November 29. This was the first wedding celebrated between a member of the British Royal Family and a foreign Princess since Alexandra of Denmark was married to Edward VII—then Prince of Wales—in 1863. Above is a photograph of the wedding certificate of the Duke and Duchess of Kent, and on the right, a snapshot of the couple taken on their honeymoon.

Photos : Topical

P

Photo : Times

On December 25, the King broadcast a message to the Empire, as he sat in his study at Sandringham. This photograph shows His Majesty seated in front of the microphone. His stirring message is reproduced on the opposite page.

The King's Christmas Message

O N this Christmas Day I send to all my people everywhere my Christmas greeting. The day, with its hallowed memories, is the Festival of the Family. I would like to think that you who are listening to me now, in whatever part of the world you may be, and all the peoples of this Realm and Empire, are bound to me and to one another by the spirit of one great family. The Queen and I were deeply moved by the manner in which this spirit was manifested a month ago at the marriage of our dear son and daughter.

My desire and hope is that the same spirit may become ever stronger in its hold and wider in its range. The world is still restless and troubled. The clouds are lifting, but we have still our own anxieties to meet. I am convinced that if we meet them in the spirit of one family we shall overcome them, for then private and party interests will be controlled by care for the whole community.

It is as members of one family that we shall to-day, and always, remember those other members of it who are suffering from sickness or from the lack of work and hope ; and we shall be ready to do our utmost to befriend them.

I send a special greeting to the peoples of my Dominions overseas. Through them the family has become a fellowship of free nations, and they have carried into their own homes the memories and traditions of the Mother Country. With them I bear in my heart to-day the peoples of my far-distant Colonies. The bond of the one spirit knows no barriers of space.

If my voice reaches any of the peoples of India, let it bring the assurance of my constant care for them, and of my desire that they, too, may ever more fully realise and value their own place in the unity of the one family.

May I add very simply and sincerely that if I may be regarded as in some true sense the head of this great and widespread family, sharing its life and sustained by its affection, this will be a full reward for the long and sometimes anxious labours of my reign of well-nigh five-and-twenty years ?

As I sit in my own home I am thinking of the great multitudes who are listening to my voice, whether they be in British homes or in far-off regions of the world. For you all, and especially for your children, I wish a Happy Christmas. I commend you to " The Father of Whom every family in heaven and on earth is named." God bless you all.

PRINCIPAL EVENTS OF 1934

JAN. 8. Stavisky, French financier, found shot.

,, 9 Street rioting in Paris.

,, 15. Earthquake in India, heavy death roll·

,, 19. Prince George departs for South Africa.

27. M. Chautemp's Ministry resigned.

FEB. 7. Monsieur Doumergue accepts French Premiership.

,, 12. Civil war in Austria—machine-guns fire on workers' tenements in Vienna.

,, 17. King of the Belgians killed while mountaineering.

,, 22. Funeral of the King of the Belgians.

,, 23. King Leopold III proclaimed in Brussels.

,, 23. Death of Sir Edward Elgar.

MAR. 1. Pu Yi enthroned as 1st Emperor of Manchukuo.

17. Cambridge win Boat Race.

APR. 11. Death of Sir Gerald du Maurier, famous actor-manager.

,, 28. Manchester City beat Portsmouth at Wembley in Cup Final, by two goals to one.

MAY 8. Attempt to assassinate Sir John Anderson, Governor of Bengal.

,, 12. U.S.A. golfers win the Walker Cup.

,, 15. *Olympic* collides with Nantucket Lightship.

JUNE 6. The Maharajah of Rajpipla's Windsor Lad wins the Derby.

,, 8. England v. Australia Test Matches began.

,, 10. Death of Frederick Delius, blind composer.

,, 29. Henry Cotton wins British Open Golf Championship.

JULY 6. F. J. Perry wins Men's Singles Championship at Wimbledon.

,, 7. Miss Dorothy Round wins Women's Singles Championship at Wimbledon.

,, 18. King opens Mersey Tunnel.

,, 19. Government announce 500 new 'planes for R.A.F.

,, 23. John Dillinger, America's "Public Enemy No. 1" shot dead.

,, 25. Dr. Dollfuss assassinated by Nazis.

,, 27. Fierce fighting in Austria between Heimwehr and Nazis.

AUG. 2. Death of President von Hindenburg. Hitler appointed President by Cabinet decree.

,, 13. Prince Gonzalo, youngest son of ex-King Alphonso dies after motor accident.

., 22. Australia regain the "Ashes."

,, 27. "Silence Zone" introduced in London.

SEPT. 3. Miss Evangeline Booth elected General of the Salvation Army.

,, 6. B.B.C. Droitwich Station opened.

,, 8. Over 130 lives lost in *Morro Castle* fire disaster.

,, 22. Over 260 miners lose their lives in Gresford Colliery disaster.

,, 25. *Rainbow* (U.S.A.) wins the America Cup.

,, 26. Cunard-White Star liner " No. 534 " christened *Queen Mary* and launched by the Queen on the Clyde.

,, 28. Railway disaster at Warrington.

OCT. 9. King Alexander I of Yugoslavia and Monsieur Barthou, French Foreign Minister, assassinated at Marseilles.

,, 10. Peter the Second proclaimed King in Belgrade.

,, 15. Death of M. Poincare.

,, 23. Scott and Black win England-Australia £10,000 Air Race (2 days, 22 hours 58 minutes).

NOV. 7. President Roosevelt gains sweeping victory in United States Congressional elections.

,, 8. Monsieur Doumergue, French Premier, resigns.

,, 13. Betting and Lotteries Bill passed in House of Commons.

,, 23. Death of Sir Arthur Pinero, British dramatist.

., 29. Wedding of the Duke of Kent and Princess Marina of Greece.

DEC. 6. Thousands of Hungarians expelled from Yugoslavia.

,, 17. First convoy of British troops leave for the Saar for guard duties during plebiscite.

,, 29. Japan gives two years' notice to end the Washington Naval Treaty.

COMPULSORY DRIVING TESTS

The polling day of the Saar plebiscite was on January 13, and by an enormous majority, the people of the Saar elected their land to become German territory. The district was formally handed over to Germany on March 1, and this photograph shows Herr Adolf Hitler, who had arrived on that day by aeroplane, taking the salute during the celebrations.

Photo : Topical

On January 17, Mr. Lloyd George, who had been living in semi-retirement, outlined his proposals in a speech at Bangor for his " New Deal." His proposals were by special request subsequently submitted to the Government. This portrait of the father of the House of Commons, was taken at his home at Churt where he has a model farm of which he is proud.

On March 7, Sir Malcolm Campbell set up a new record on Daytona beach of 276.816 m.p.h. This photograph sho

Photo : Topical

...alcolm just before he left England, and his re-built Bluebird, fitted with a 2,500-h.p. Rolls-Royce Schneider engine.

On September 22, 1934, occurred one of the worst disasters in mining history, when nearly 300 miners lost their lives in Gresford Colliery in Wales. After the explosion which caused the tragedy, the gas fumes were so deadly that 254 bodies still in the pit could not be rescued, and the pit had to be sealed up. On March 7 volunteers who had been especially trained, descended into the death pit to report conditions. Here is one of these men, who risked his life to reclaim his comrades' bodies. Complete with gas mask and other special apparatus, he is seen receiving last-minute instructions.

Photo : " Weekly Illustrated "

The towering figure of Christ by the famous sculptor, Jacob Epstein, has aroused a storm of controversy among critics and public alike. Some see in this massive stone statue a majestic representation of " The Man of Sorrows "—an inspiring symbol of all that is noble and wonderful in man. Others, who have not hesitated to attack it furiously, by every means in their power say that they can see in it nothing but ugliness, vulgarity and even profanity. There are others, too, who gaze on it frankly bewildered, neither comprehending its greatness nor criticising its apparent crudity.

On March 16, Herr Hitler announced a new Conscription Act. The next day Sunday was Memorial Day in honour of German soldiers who fell in the War. The picture shows Herr Hitler at the Kroll Opera House during the ceremony.

(Picture by wire.) Sir John Simon, British Foreign Secretary, and Mr. Anthony Eden, Lord Privy Seal, with Herr Hitler at the Chancellery in Berlin, where on March 25 they began an important series of discussions on the European situation.

Photos : *Topical*

Early this year Sir Kingsley Wood, Postmaster-General, announced that a committee would be formed to advise in the development of television, and that in the autumn a National Television Service will operate, controlled by the B.B.C.

Before the arduous programme of the Jubilee celebrations their Majesties took a holiday at Eastbourne. This picture shows H.M. the Queen during her stay at Eastbourne, leaving the Parish Church at Alfriston after an informal visit.

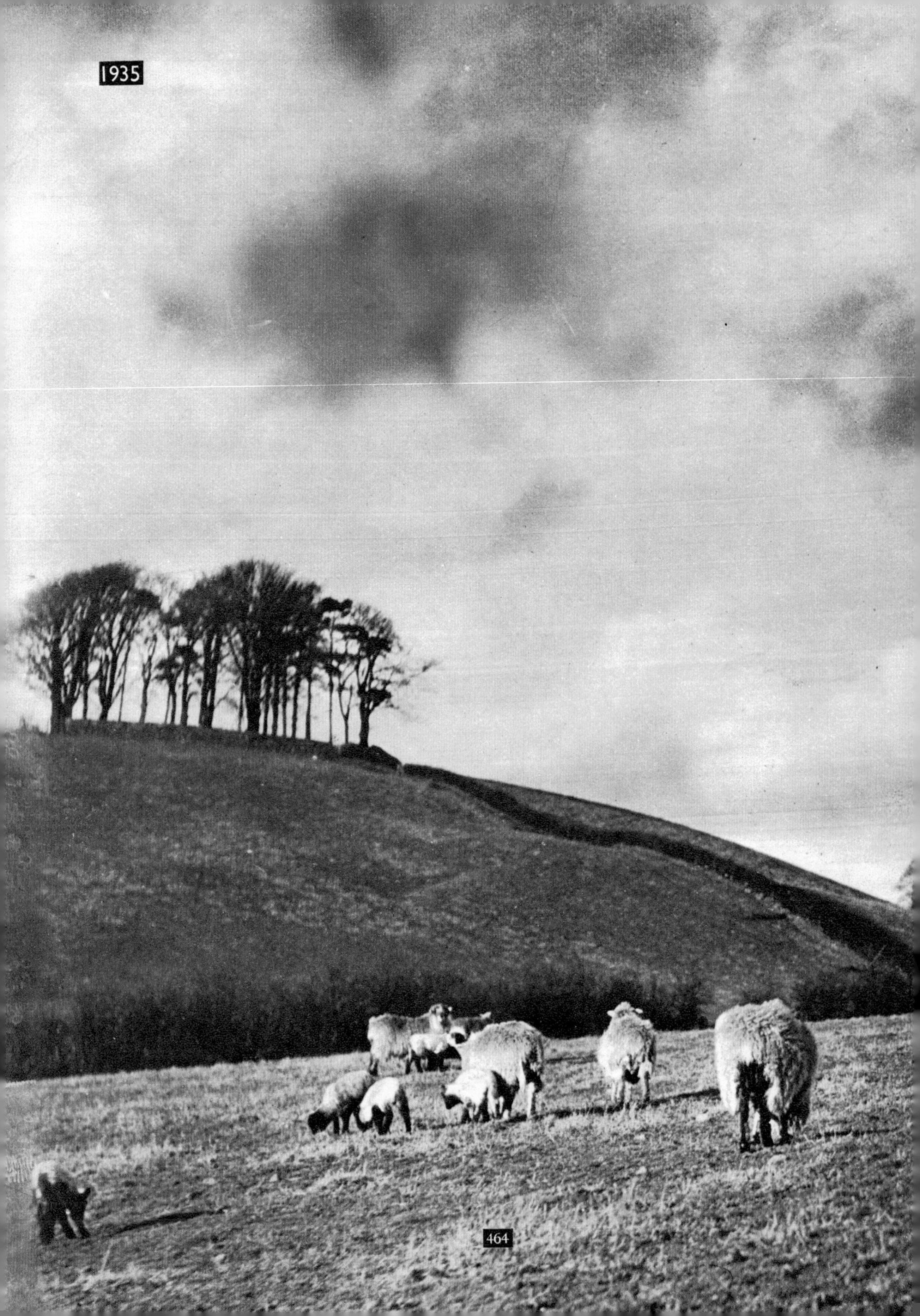

Here beats the Heart of England

IN these quiet green pastures, "under an English heaven," is the everlasting symbol of that peace and beauty which all mankind desires. Even the silence here speaks of a great content, of faith in simple things. And set beyond the tree-fringed hillock is the horizon of Hope—hope that the years to come may be rich and fertile, free and peaceful in the green fields of the motherland that gave us birth.

Photo: Fox

STYLE and SPEED
through 25 years

SO, on the threshold of new wonders yet beyond the power of prophecy, we complete our pictured story of the most eventful quarter-century of all time. It has been a story of vast changes, a study in startling contrasts. But through all the intensely interesting panorama of these twenty-five years, it is probable that no changes have been so marked as those connected with our fashions in dress and our methods of travel. For this reason the two supplements that follow deal in greater detail with these two important phases of our national life than was possible in the preceding record of events.

If a Rip Van Winkle of those distant Edwardian days of 1910 were to wake to-day, these changes in style and speed would surely amaze him most.

How he would rub his eyes at the transformation that clothes alone have wrought in the daily scene. The awe-inspiring dignity of the City man's silk hat or high-crowned bowler, stiff upstanding collar and abundant whiskers has given place to such free-and-easy comfort that he would think the very foundations of Throgmorton Street in danger. For even when, in more abandoned moments, your Edwardian sported the natty boater or the nattier striped blazer, those whiskers warned against undue frivolity.

As for the ladies, if our sleeper woke with misgivings at the sight of soft collars and plus-fours, he would be utterly bewildered by the change from the feminine fashions of his day. Huge " picture hats " loaded down with artificial flowers, hour-glass waists, skirts that trailed in the dust and were lifted at crossings so as not to expose more than an inch or so of woollen-stockinged ankle—that was woman's dress as he would remember it. Even at tennis, the ground-length skirts were worn. And when the daring girls, in mob caps and costumes each with more than enough material for a modern frock, splashed together in the sea, real gentlemen looked the other way. And yet, slim, modern miss in your glistening, backless swim suit, do not laugh ! For, by these brave pioneers gained you this freedom.

But it is in our modes of travel that the almost miraculous changes of these years are most obvious. With the passing of the hansom cab a picturesque page of memories was turned, the like of which will never be written again. The hansom, more than any other vehicle of its time, marks the end of an era—an era of stage-door Johnnies and gas-lit streets. Contemporary of the four-horse " brake " and the open phaeton, it clatters over the cobbles and into history. It left the stage set for what in truth can be called, as far as travel is concerned, a " brave new world."

From the time when a car ride meant dressing up with fearsome goggles and flowing veils, we have moved to a new age of silent, almost incredible swiftness.

On the straight, new broad highways, our traffic problems are but growing pains. Our Rip Van Winkle staring aghast at a great passenger 'plane zooming high in the skies down to a perfect landing at Croydon or reading amazed of over 400 m.p.h. speed bids, might realise that more clearly than we do ourselves. Momentous as are the changes marked by the Jubilee of 1935, it is certain that they are little more than an inkling of still greater changes yet to come.

Photo : Topical

SEEN IN THE PARK—1910 !

ARMOUR PLATE ELEGANCE!

THOUGH an immense amount of tailoring went to the making of ladies' dresses in 1910, the result to modern eyes seems strangely lacking in smartness. Only in habits or blouses and skirts was anything like simplicity of line achieved. Left, is a group of that year's fashions, while below is a view of Richmond Horse Show. This was, for women, an era of armour plating, corseting, inaccessible hooks and eyes and skirts that trailed in dust and mud, and required endless brushing. Whether the results achieved were worth all this effort it may be left to the modern eye to judge.

Photos: Cen. Press

OPEN ROAD

AND ALMOST

CLOSED SEA!

CYCLING was in its heyday when King George came to the throne, but it went out of favour as a fashionable recreation and has only in the last few years regained its popularity. The lady on the right is wearing a dashing tailored costume smartly finished off by the mannish shirt-blouse and tie. Notice her partner's low handlebars and single brake.

Below is a group of bathing belles from an early film, wearing the very last word in beach attire. The athletic effect is somewhat spoiled by the tights and laced boots—and surely taffeta (worn by the fourth girl from the left) is not the best material to bathe in!

Photo : Topical

THE
PRE-WAR
YEARS

ABOVE is a river scene in 1911 where the huge hats are piled with flowers like miniature gardens. On the left is a costume seen at Ascot the previous year. Notice the huge bird's-nest turban of tulle, straw and feathers. Nearly everybody was wearing black just then in mourning for King Edward. On the right is a juvenile summer fashion which typifies an era when children were muffled and swathed in starched muslins and cambrics, with floppy hats kept on by an elastic band, that pinched the wearer's chin—when it was not being sucked!

HATS
IN THEIR
HEYDAY!

IN 1910 and 1911 hats were perhaps bigger than they had been for over a century. Every theatre had its notice requesting ladies to remove their hats—and one enterprising manager actually hired a lady to attend every matinee in a huge erection like the example on the right, which she refused to remove. Protests were made by the audience, the case got into the papers and thus indirectly advertised the play! Below is a street scene in 1910, and in the bottom right corner is an Ascot fashion of 1911. Notice the hangbag hung from a chain in front.

Photo: Cen. Press

Photo: Topical

471

LADIES
of the
CLASSIC LINE

By 1912 the " classic line " had developed into the styles illustrated on the left. Notice the open sleeves laced with braid, and the combination of spotted " transparency," braid, ornaments, brooches and neck-lace on the bodice. Cartwheel hats with wide shallow crowns were fashionable, necessitating dressing the hair in puffs and folds—and in some cases supplementing its bulk by " bird-cages " and " horse-tails." Below is an athletic young lady of 1912 attempting the high jump in a gym-costume of the period. A lifetime of long skirts has made her grasp her tunic from force of habit to raise it off the ground, even as she jumps.

THE ATHLETIC
YOUNG LADY

Photos " Daily Mirror "

ALPACA
IN
OXFORD STREET

ON the right is a daring bid for light clothing in hot weather, snapped in Oxford Street in 1912. Although light flannel, alpaca and even tussore suits for men are common enough to-day, such a costume was an even more startling reform at that time than any of the examples illustrated in the picture at the foot of page 483. Below is a happy group on Hampstead Heath. The cutaway or three-quarter length coat was then being worn—and, of course, feathers in nearly every hat! These ladies are out to enjoy themselves—it being Bank Holiday—but it looks like a rough day for the hats and the feathers.

'APPY
'AMPSTEAD

Photo: Cen. Press

Photo: Topical

THE HAREM SKIRT

*B*ELOW is a characteristically oriental fashion of 1912. The harem skirt arrived—but did not stay for long. On the right is a yachting costume of 1913 seen at Cowes. *Inset :* A lace-trimmed hat considered smart in 1914.

THIS WAS CONSIDERED SMART !

EARLY
WAR
FASHIONS

*T*HE French model, complete with cloak and parasol, is typical of the odd, half-tailored fashions of the early war years. Later, lines became more severe. Hats, too, took on a more military appearance. The contrast is shown on this page between the rose-and-ribbon garlanded example in the top right-hand corner and the hussar-like toque on the left. On the right is a family group seen at a race meeting.

Photos : S. & G.

WHAT THEY WORE IN THE WAR !

AS the War continued, fashions varied from a semi-military smartness—as illustrated by the check tweed costume shown above—and almost orientally feminine styles for evening. One wore one's best when one went out with a soldier. On the right is a bathing-belle of the period; above, an evening ensemble.

TOUCH OF VARIETY!

THOUGH not exactly modish, the picture above represents a definite war-time fashion—when women adopted, as far as possible, the uniforms of the men's trades they had taken over. The Cossack-like fashion illustrated in the top right corner was common during the first two years of the War, remaining in favour until Russia withdrew from the combat. Below is an informal snapshot taken on the river in 1917.

Photo: Topical

"AFTER THE WAR WAS OVER"

THE post-War slump created a few "economical" fashions of which one type is represented by the hand-painted taffeta evening dress on the left. The "sensible" one-strap shoes—black worn with light stockings—had the effect of making the feet look very big—but it was fashionable. A contrast in bathing styles is afforded by the other pictures—but perhaps the one on the right was not intended by its owner ever to get wet!

Photo: Cen. Press

BOBBED hair, which after the War assumed many and various styles, of which one is illustrated on the right, was characteristic among the younger set. Dresses were narrow and long, with a very low waist and a tendency toward sweeping lines from neck to hem. At the bottom of the page is a lace-brimmed hat of 1921. The odd bits and pieces that dangled from it were considered very smart.

Photo : Topical

Photo : Cen. Press

Photo : G.P.U.

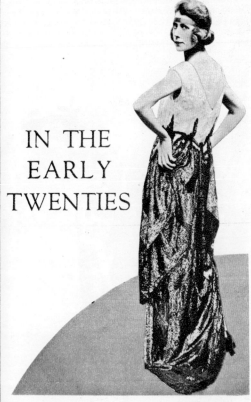

IN THE EARLY TWENTIES

THE REBUFF TO THE MUFF!

DURING the early 'twenties muffs were going out. Women no longer walked about with their hands thrust behind a snarling mask complete with teeth and eyes and four or five tails. Above is an example of the severer type of muff then fashionable, together with a smart fur coat seen at Ascot. Hats, though smaller, became congested with flowers, like the one resembling a sea-anemone illustrated on the right. In the evening, trains and slightly *bouffant* effects were popular, though to modern eyes the dress illustrated at the top right corner seems to have little or no "line." Notice (*right*) the ribbon *bandeau*

WOULD
YOU
BELIEVE IT?

TOWARDS the end of the 'twenties skirts began to get shorter and shorter, culminating in the styles shown here where the knee is only just covered. At the same time the shingle (seen in the top left corner) which followed after the "bob"—a fashion that originated during the War—became more and more severe, and eventually the "Eton crop" (*top centre*) became the rage —a fashion only suitable for those with well-defined profiles and prettily shaped ears!

Q

OXFORD BAGS
HAVE THEIR DAY

ABOVE are examples of " Oxford bags " which, though " freaks " or " stunts " in themselves, have influenced the width of the modern trouser. *Top left :* A straw development of the " bowler." In the bottom left corner is a pyjama mode in a large and vivid pattern not to be recommended to any but the very slim. *Below* is a close-fitting hat designed to show off the latest style of hairdressing.

HERE'S ANOTHER DRESS LENGTH!

BY the 'thirties, skirts were becoming longer. The growing popularity of cruising started new fashions in evening and beach wear; while, with the general tendency towards greater ease in clothing, the Men's Dress Reform Movement had come into being in 1929 and now continues to produce each year more original designs for day and evening wear. *Top left:* Feathers and spots were fashionable at this period. *Top right:* First, the "curate's" hat, and coat designed on Chinese lines with severe neck line; then a beach ensemble of heavy baggy trousers and enormous "sunbathing" straw hat. *Right* is a glimpse of experimental male modes at a Dress Reform Dance.

THRILLS AND FLOUNCES!

FASHION designers had decreed a return to frills and
flounces in the summer of 1930. But they had reckoned
without the weather. The first day of Ascot, where all the
latest chiffons and delicate wide-brimmed hats were displayed,
the rain poured in a steady deluge that ruined thousands of
pounds' worth of summer models and definitely affected the sale
of "spoilable" frocks. Above is an "Ascot fashion" as seen
that year. *Right* are two characteristic modes of 1934—the
severe tailored coat and small, round "Princess Marina" hats.

Two Ascot fashions that were *not* damaged by the rain, showing a tendency to return to the flowing lines of 1914.

Women are no longer content to paddle and splash.   Hence their bathing costumes are now streamlined " swim-suits."

THE AGE OF SPEED

Photo : " Daily Herald "

In 1910 the hansom cab was a popular form of conveyance in London. Business men in the city, theatre folk and the Bohemian life of London still were using the " hansom." The driver conversed with his " fare " through a trap in the roof.

Photo : Topical

In 1910 the horse 'bus also was still a familiar feature, although the early motor omnibuses were then on the roads. It was no uncommon experience for motor 'buses to break down and for the passengers to be transferred to horse 'buses.

An old four-wheel cab, popularly known at that period as the " growler." This type of vehicle was in more general use for conveying passengers with luggage. The " hansom " cab was regarded as the " speed " vehicle of that period.

CARRIAGE FOLK OF YESTERDAY

AMONG the many types of private vehicles in use at this time was the Brougham, seating two or more persons and drawn by one or two horses. This imposing carriage was inspired and named after Lord Brougham, the famous Lord Chancellor, who himself designed a vehicle of this type and had it specially made for his own use. As a " closed " carriage it gained great popularity. Later its general shape and design were included in some of the early models of the mechanically propelled cars.

The four-wheel Phaeton continued to remain in favour with those who could afford to possess their own private vehicles. Above one shown in a queue on London Bridge. It is fitted with a collapsible hood for the wet weather.

NEW "HORSES" FOR OLD

Photo : L.P.T.B.

Above is one of the last pair-horse trams—the average speed of which was 6 to 7 miles per hour. It was the forerunner of the big, luxurious and speedy electric models of to-day.

Photo : Sedgwick, Ltd.

Although horse-drawn vehicles were to be seen in plenty, the year of 1910 saw the beginning of what could be regarded as popular motoring. The early cars provided even more thrills than the streamlined sports cars of to-day. Above can be seen an elegant turn-out of the period, a 10-h.p. Rolls Royce with two cylinders and one spare wheel!

LONDON CELEBRATES THE CORONATION

Photo : Topical

Top : The scene in Parliament Street in 1911 on the occasion of the Coronation of King George V. It is interesting to compare this " traffic jam " with others depicted in this section. *Below :* A typical view of river pleasure craft going through Boulter's Lock on the River Thames. reminiscent of what now seems those halcyon days " just before the War."

Here is a view of Regent Street in 1912—long before traffic had become a problem. Although petrol-driven vehicles were fast ousting the horse-drawn types, traffic signals, pedestrian crossings and other devices introduced for the safety of road users, were as yet unneccessary and far from the minds of the public. Contrast this picture with the one on page 508.

In 1913 you could take your choice between horse and petrol. For trips by road to the coast and for week-end " outings " the horse brake was an accepted means of travel. This picture, taken at a starting point, is typical of the popularity of this type of conveyance. As can be seen, some of the brakes have framework on which is placed a weatherproof canvas covering.

Excursions by motor in public conveyances were beginning to be widely patronised. 1913 saw many forms of char-a-bancs—as they came to be known—and companies were being formed to run regular services. The one in the above picture shows the Southdown Motor Service which did a tour of the Lakes from Brighton.

TRAVELLING TO THE DERBY

The road to the Derby is outstanding for its many and varying modes of travel. The procession to the course on Derby Day provides an example, as nothing else does, of practically every variety of vehicle in use at the time. The scene above shows the road to the Downs in 1911; that below, a Derby Day party arriving in style in the fateful summer of 1914.

In 1914 many of the small towns and villages were still unaffected by motor travel of any kind, and on market day from Bishop Thornton to Knaresborough and Ripon in Yorkshire, an old public horse 'bus served the district, carrying passengers to and from these towns. It was and still is known in the district as "Webster's Chariot," and to prove that the local folk prefer to travel by this ancient conveyance instead of "they motors," this horse 'bus is still in service.

At this period the privately-owned motor-car was beginning to become the proud possession of those who could afford this luxury form of travel. Cars—as can be seen in this illustration—were not as yet being built for either comfort or speed.

Photo : *Sport and General*

During the War years there was an acute petrol shortage and all types of motor conveyances had to resort to the "gas-bag." Here is a picture of a taxi cab of that period showing the specially fitted roof and the "gas-bag" device.

THROUGH SLEEPING BRITAIN. A striking picture of the " Night Scotsman " leaving King's Cross on its nightly

trek North of nearly 400 miles. This is the sister of the "Flying Scotsman" which makes the journey during the daytime.

' TAXI "—TAKE YOUR CHOICE

Photo : Topical

After the war the street taxi had become a national institution as a popular mode of conveyance. Above is an illustration of an old type of street taxi, and, below, the latest thing in river taxis—a streamlined motor-boat on the Thames.

Photo : " Daily Herald "

The tram, having to compete with its more mobile sister the motor 'bus, was modernised and brought up-to-date. Every day thousands of workers pour into the city from outlying districts, and return home by tram. Here is a typical "hold-up" scene on Blackfriars Bridge, showing an unbroken line of trams right across the bridge.

Photo : " Daily Herald "

FROM THE SEVEN SEAS. No story of transport would be complete without a photograph of London's mammoth docks, the hub of the Empire's maritime trade, the haven of ships of every nationality. It is seldom that the camera

matches so nearly the skill of the great artist in catching the spirit of London's river as it does in this striking illustration showing a typical scene in the Royal Albert Dock with liners, barges, tugs and sailing vessels side by side.

TRAFFIC EYES—

ABOVE AND BELOW

CONTROLLING the traffic from the air and on the ground. The auto-gyro enables the traffic police to locate congestion in the main thoroughfares. Reports are sent by wireless to those controlling traffic below.

Mediterranean Magic.   A beautiful camera study of one of the Imperial Airways "Scipio" Flying Boats on a night flight.   This type of machine is used on the Mediterranean stage of the Empire air routes.

Photo : " Flight "

Photo: "Daily Herald"

A typical scene during the rush period in the neighbourhood of Piccadilly Circus. The stream of traffic is seen sweeping into Regent Street. What a contrast to the clear and peaceful atmosphere of this same spot in 1912 as shown on page 494.

Photo: "Weekly Illustrated"

108 M.P.H.! A unique view of the L.N.E.R. locomotive "Papyrus" leaving King's Cross with the train that broke all records on the London-Newcastle and return journey on March 5, 1935. It first came into service in February, 1928.

HAPPINESS ON WHEELS

Top : The modern miss, complete with shorts or plus fours, carries on the cycling tradition that her great-grandfather introduced.   Here is a typical week-end Club " meet " preparatory to a long run to the country or seaside.

" A bicycle made for three !" A happy family party setting off in search of fresh air and happiness on a modern tandem, a machine which is becoming very popular. It is estimated that in Great Britain to-day there are nearly ten million cyclists.

Photo : " Daily Herald "

The last word in traffic control.   Belisha Beacons, traffic lights, pedestrian safety lanes, and now—the 30 m.p.h. limit in built-up areas.   Here is a corner of Trafalgar Square showing traffic and pedestrians responding to the new devices.

Photo: Maycock, Odhams Press Ltd.

LITTLE MAN WHAT NOW?

THE SERVICE IN ST. PAUL'S

TO

"My Very Dear People"

HIS MAJESTY'S BROADCAST
FROM BUCKINGHAM PALACE
ON JUBILEE DAY, MAY 6, 1935

AT the close of this memorable day I must speak to my people everywhere. Yet how can I express what is in my heart? As I passed this morning through cheering multitudes to and from St. Paul's Cathedral, as I thought there of all that these twenty-five years have brought to me and to my country and my Empire, how could I fail to be most deeply moved? Words cannot express my thoughts and feelings.

I can only say to you, my very dear people, that the Queen and I thank you from the depth of our hearts for all the loyalty and—may I say?—the love with which this day and always you have surrounded us. I dedicate myself anew to your service for the years that may still be given to me.

I look back on the past with thankfulness to God. My people and I have come through great trials and difficulties together. They are not over. In the midst of this day's rejoicing I grieve to think of the numbers of my people who are still without work. We owe to them, and not least to those who are suffering from any form of disablement, all the sympathy and help that we can give. I hope that during this Jubilee Year all who can will do their utmost to find them work and bring them hope.

Other anxieties may be in store. But I am persuaded that with God's help they may all be overcome, if we meet them with confidence, courage, and unity. So I look forward to the future with faith and hope.

It is to the young that the future belongs. I trust that through the Fund inaugurated by my dear son, the Prince of Wales, to commemorate this year, many of them throughout this country may be helped in body, mind, and character to become useful citizens.

To the children I would like to send a special message. Let me say this to each of them whom my words may reach—The King is speaking to *you*. I ask you to remember that in days to come you will be the citizens of a great Empire. As you grow up, always keep this thought before you; and when the time comes be ready and proud to give to your country the service of your work, your mind, and your heart.

I have been greatly touched by all the greetings which have come to me to-day from my Dominions and Colonies, from India and from this home country. My heart goes out to all who may be listening to me now wherever you may be—here at home in town or village, or in some far-off corner of the Empire or it may be on the high seas.

Let me end my words to you with those which Queen Victoria used after her Diamond Jubilee thirty-eight years ago. No words could more truly or simply express my own deep feeling now : " From my heart I thank my beloved people. May God bless them."

Photo: Keystone

From all over the world came crowds to witness the Jubilee. All wheeled vehicles were diverted in the main streets after nine o'clock every evening so that visitors might view the decorations without danger from traffic. The picture above shows the vast crowds in Oxford Street, London, on the evening before the Jubilee Procession. Below is a view of the spectators who took their positions on the route and spent the night there, sleeping, in some cases, where they sat.

Photo: Photopress

CITY
OF
LIGHT
AND
BEAUTY

Photo: Fox

*T*HE principal centres at night presented a magnificent spectacle to Jubilee sightseers. Many of the most stately buildings and monuments were floodlit every evening. The picture on the left shows how the illuminations revealed the rare beauty of King Henry VII's Chapel, Westminster Abbey. Below is a view of the Thames, with Thames House and Imperial Chemical House in the background.

Photo: Topical

THE ROYAL PROCESSION

CHEERED by a mighty throng of loyal citizens, the Jubilee Procession passed through the London streets on the morning of May 6. Brilliant weather prevailed throughout the day. Many famous personalities took part in the Procession, including members of the Royal Family, the Prime Minister (Mr. Ramsay MacDonald), the Lord Chancellor (Lord Sankey), the Speaker (Captain Fitzroy), and the Dominion Premiers.

Right : The Prince of Wales, the Queen of Norway, and the Duke of Gloucester.

Below : The Duke and Duchess of York, accompanied by the two little princesses, Elizabeth and Margaret Rose.

Photo : Topical

Photo : Topical

Photo : Topical

Photo : Topical

THE KING AND QUEEN DRIVE IN STATE TO ST. PAUL'S

ABOVE is a picture of the impressive scene outside Buckingham Palace as Their Majesties started on their drive to St. Paul's Cathedral for the Thanksgiving Service, which commenced at 11.30 a.m. on May 6. The entire route was densely crowded with spectators anxious to catch a glimpse of the King and Queen. Bright sunshine and picturesque uniforms added to the splendour of the occasion. On the left, the King is seen receiving the Pearl Sword of the City from the Lord Mayor of London at Temple Bar. This sword is the traditional symbol of the City's independence. His Majesty returns it to the Lord Mayor after having touched the hilt.

Photo: *British International P.P.A.*

Over 4,000 people were assembled in St. Paul's Cathedral on the morning of May 6, at the Service of Thanksgiving for "the protection afforded to the King's Majesty during the twenty-five years of his auspicious reign." The King and Queen, and other members of the Royal Family, are seen in the picture. The service was conducted by the Archbishop of Canterbury, assisted by the Bishop of London, the Dean of St. Paul's, Canon Alexander and the Rev. M. F. Foxell. The Rev. Dr. S. H. Berry represented the Free Churches. This memorable and impressive event was broadcast.

THIS remarkable photograph, taken from the roof of Buckingham Palace, shows the Royal Procession returning along the Mall—a bird's-eye view of the most impressive State pageant of modern times. In the foreground is the Queen Victoria Memorial, which served as a grand stand on this occasion. St. James's Park is on the right of the picture, while the dome of St. Paul's Cathedral and other landmarks can be seen in the distance.

Photo : Topical

Photo : Topical

AFTER THE PROCESSION

*A*FTER the return of the Procession from St. Paul's Cathedral, a cheering crowd assembled outside Buckingham Palace. The picture above shows members of the Royal Family acknowledging this spontaneous expression of loyalty and affection. *Left to right :* The Duke of York, Princess Royal, the King, Princess Margaret Rose, Earl of Harewood, Hon. Gerald Lascelles, Princess Elizabeth, Viscount Lascelles, the Queen, Duke of Gloucester, Duchess of Kent, Duke of Kent and Duchess of York.

*B*Y pressing a button in Buckingham Palace, shortly before 10 p.m., the King lit the huge Jubilee bonfire in Hyde Park. On the left is a view of this fire, which was the first of a chain of 2,000 bonfires that flared from point to point throughout Great Britain on the night of May 6.

Photo: *Photographic News Agencies Ltd.*

Their Majesties receiving the addresses of congratulation from the Lords and Commons in Westminster Hall on May 9.

Photo: Topical

In Wales and Scotland the Silver Jubilee was celebrated amid scenes of great enthusiasm. The picture above shows the Prince of Wales arriving on May 11 at Cathays Park, Cardiff, where 100,000 people watched him lay a wreath on the Welsh National War Memorial. Below, the Duchess of York is seen releasing pigeons which conveyed the greetings of the citizens of Edinburgh to the King on May 11. The Duchess was accompanied by the Duke of York (seen on the left.)

Photo: Fox

Photo : Topical

Throughout the country, everyone entered into the holiday spirit which marked Jubilee Day—both in the heart of the city, and in the outlying districts. *Above :* Inhabitants of a gaily decorated street near Blackfriars Road, London, taking part in the celebrations, a scene typical of the carnival spirit prevailing everywhere. *Below :* Immense crowds gathered outside Buckingham Palace night after night during Jubilee week, waiting for the King to appear on the balcony.

Photo : Sport & General

Photo: Topical

THE KING VISITS THE LONDON SUBURBS. A happy scene at the children's Jubilee Tea-Party in Battersea on May 6. *Inset :* A glimpse of the King and Queen during their drive through the East End of London on May 25.

Photo: Sport & General

Children as well as grown-ups joined in the Jubilee festivities.   The above picture shows a vast crowd of London school-children, chosen from districts which the King would be unable to visit, cheering their Majesties as they left Buckingham Palace for a drive to North London on May 11.   *Below :* The King and Queen acknowledging the children's greetings as the Royal Carriage passed along Constitution Hill.   More than seventy-five thousand children were present.

Photo: Topical

When the pageantry and mirth of the Jubilee are but fading memories, among the deep impressions remaining in the minds of the British people will be the silent grandeur of the great floodlit buildings. The above picture shows a typical sight of Jubilee week—the beautiful *façade* of the Middlesex Guildhall, Westminster, in the mellow glow of the illuminations.